Stoicism

The Timeless Wisdom to Living a Good life

Develop Grit, Build Confidence, and Find Inner Peace

Stoicism

PUBLISHED BY: James W. Williams

© Copyright 2019 - All rights reserved.

The content contained within this book may not be reproduced, duplicated or transmitted without direct written permission from the author or the publisher.

Under no circumstances will any blame or legal responsibility be held against the publisher, or author, for any damages, reparation, or monetary loss due to the information contained within this book. Either directly or indirectly.

Legal Notice:

This book is copyright protected. This book is only for personal use. You cannot amend, distribute, sell, use, quote or paraphrase any part, or the content within this book, without the consent of the author or publisher.

Disclaimer Notice:

Please note the information contained within this document is for educational and entertainment purposes only. All effort has been executed to present accurate, up to date, and reliable, complete information. No warranties of any kind are declared or implied. Readers acknowledge that the author is not engaging in the rendering of legal, financial, medical or professional advice. The content within this book has been derived from various sources. Please consult a licensed professional before attempting any techniques outlined in this book.

By reading this document, the reader agrees that under no circumstances is the author responsible for any losses, direct or indirect, which are incurred as a result of the use of information contained within this document, including, but not limited to, — errors, omissions, or inaccuracies

James W. Williams

Table of contents

Your Free Gift.. 5
Introduction 6
Chapter One: Stoicism 101................................. 9
Chapter Two: History of Stoicism 15
Chapter Three: Early Stoicism...........................21
Chapter Four: Modern Stoicism 27
Chapter Five: The Stoic Logic........................... 33
Chapter Six: General Misconceptions About Stoicism.. 39
Chapter Seven: Stoicism in Everyday Living.... 45
Chapter Eight: The Four Cardinal Virtues of Stoicism.. 50
Chapter Nine: The Practice of Misfortune 55
Chapter Ten: The Training of Perception......... 63
Chapter Eleven: Keeping the Balance with Eupatheiai 68
Chapter Twelve: Plato's View 74
Chapter Thirteen: Memento Mori (Remember Death).. 79
Chapter Fourteen: Recognizing Limits 85
Chapter Fifteen: Journaling 90

Chapter Sixteen: Premeditatio Malorum (The Premeditation of Evil) 96

Chapter Seventeen: Amor Fati (Love Fate) 102

Chapter Eighteen: The Power to Enforce Change 108

Chapter Nineteen: Stoicism in Cognitive Behavioral Therapy 113

Chapter Twenty: Stoicism in Pain Management 121

Chapter Twenty-one: Stoicism in Growing Emotional Intelligence 129

Chapter Twenty-two: Stoic Exercises and Practices to Get You Started 134

Chapter Twenty-three: Taking Ownership of Your Life 140

Closing 145

Thank you 148

Your Free Gift

As a way of saying thanks for your purchase, I wanted to offer you a free bonus E-book called ***Bulletproof Confidence,*** exclusive to the readers of this book.
To get instant access, just go to:
https://theartofmastery.com/confidence/

Inside the book, you will discover:
- What are shyness and social anxiety, and the psychology behind them
- Simple yet powerful strategies for overcoming social anxiety
- Breakdown of the traits of what makes a confident person
- Traits you must DESTROY if you want to become confident
- Easy techniques you can implement TODAY to keep the conversation flowing
- Confidence checklist to ensure you're on the right path of self-development

Introduction

"It's time you realized that you have something in you more powerful and miraculous than the things that affect you and make you dance like a puppet."
Marcus Aurelius

I remember the very first time I encountered this quote. I was doing some online research for a project I was working on and, by chance, I stumbled on a page with this quote at the very top. I was experiencing one of the lowest points in my life. I was juggling so many projects at the same time and, as you can imagine, I was stretched thin both mentally and emotionally. My bank account was bleeding profusely as the projects took a lot of my money, too. I was tired, but I was too afraid to stop—everything I was doing at that point in time was my identity. On top of that, my dearest friend was battling cancer. If you have ever encountered cancer, you know it takes its toll on not just the person affected, but their loved ones, too. It was a dark, dark period in my life. But when I read these words by Marcus Aurelius, I felt like he'd singled me out in that moment to speak specifically to me. As a typical skeptic, I assumed it was going to be one of those rhetorical things that resonated with you, but never really had any true impact. Still, I was desperate enough to find out more. While I hate to sound cliché about this, I have to say that ever since I took that step, I have never looked back.

Stoicism is nothing like I ever thought it would be and, at the same time, it became everything I needed. And it still is, today. Exploring it took me to heights and depths of myself that I didn't even realize were there. And these were the same words uttered by a childhood friend of mine, who had served in Iraq when the crisis there was at its peak. This was a guy who, when he returned, was a shadow of himself. A lot of us tried to help him and we failed. We were so powerless in the face of what he was going through, it affected our friendship. We fell out of touch for years but in the months following my first contact with Stoicism, I ran into him during one of my travels. I did not recognize him, so he was the one that called out to me. He was very different, but in a really good way. Gone were the sunken, sleep-deprived eyes that had become his trademark. In front of me was a healthy-looking man who appeared happier than I had ever seen him in my life. It was surreal. We chatted for hours and shared our experiences, but one comment he made really stood out for me. He said, "When I came back, I was a broken man. I

Stoicism

was barely living, and my pain on a daily basis was a steady ten. And then, the Stoics found me. My pain is still a ten on most days, but my life is richer than it had ever been. Even better than the days when my pain was a one."

This book will not change the circumstances surrounding you. By the time you get to the last page, a lot may have changed, but everything will still be the same. But take this from me: If you open your heart to the truths within, I guarantee the most important change you need to happen will have occurred—and that change will be you.

Chapter One
Stoicism 101

*"The whole future lies in uncertainty:
Live immediately."*
Seneca

When you hear the words "stoic," or "Stoicism," images of a strict and austere life spring to mind. You think of a life of abstinence devoid of pleasure or any of the good things associated with "robust" living. A person who is regarded as stoic is thought of as stern, unkind, uncompromising, and un-showing of any form of human emotion. It is typically ascribed as a masculine trait, but there are women who "fit" that description as well. In general, society's perspective on the subject of Stoicism, while it is not favorable, is not negative. And when people think of Stoicism in a belief or religious context, the general perception is that it is foreign or belongs to one of these new-age philosophies.

In subsequent chapters, I will go into detail to address the misrepresentation of Stoicism in our times, but I can categorically tell you that Stoicism is not a new-age trend. As a matter of fact, elements of Stoicism are so deep-rooted in our cultures and ways of living that we are not even aware of it. Some of the most popular phrases that have become clichés are actually rooted in Stoicism, or straight-out quotes from the founders of Stoicism themselves. One of my personal favorite is "live in the moment." This not a direct Stoic quote, but it is a paraphrased echo of a popular quote from one of the great masters of Stoicism.

"True happiness is to enjoy the present, without anxious dependence upon the future, not to amuse ourselves with either hopes or fears but to rest satisfied with what we have, which is sufficient for he that is so, wants nothing. The greatest blessings of mankind are within us and within our reach. A wise man is content with his lot, whatever it may be, without wishing for what he has not."

Seneca

Compared to this lengthy quote, the four-word version seems like a stretch but here is another pop culture phrase that is 100% Stoic. "Luck is what happens when preparation meets opportunity." You must have heard this, or a version of it, at least once in your life. My point is, the concept of Stoicism has been a part of the fabric of our society for as long as time itself. But the conscious practice of it is what has become a novelty for us. That said, what exactly is

Stoicism? And is it really relevant for our time and era?

In very simple terms, Stoicism is a way of life that extols the virtue of rooting one's happiness in their own behavior, as opposed to depending on the world as the source of one's happiness. Life is a complicated tangle of events that occur to us in series. These events trigger emotions that range from anger to zealousness. There is no "off switch" that can guarantee these events will never occur. As humans, we often convince ourselves that we will have wholesomeness, happiness, and peace in our lives only when certain events happen.

If you could land that perfect job, or if you could get a raise. If you could make more money, or if you could find that one person that completes you, or if you could have a baby. The list goes on and on. Without realizing it, we postpone our happiness with this kind of thinking. The idea that true happiness can be found in anywhere or anything but ourselves sends us on an eternal quest to locate it. Despite the harm this brings to us, we romanticize these quests, adopting social clichés that have no factual relevance to what we are going through—just so we can justify our choices.

We ascribe titles to ourselves to feel like we are truly on a journey of purpose. The "goal getter"

Stoicism has a set of mantras to keep us on the trail of our holy grail. Modern thought leaders echo our feelings with equal fervor, egging us on to our destinations. And, more often than not, we arrive at these destinations. We get what we want. We snag the trophy. But we're frequently disappointed by what we have. The man or woman of our dreams is not so charming, after all. The promotion we worked so hard for is fast becoming a nightmare. And money cannot really buy you happiness.

This realization does not stop us on our tracks, however. Instead, we simply fall back on old patterns—we just put new labels on them. "Maybe if you had a travel job, or maybe if you set up shop in a niche industry." The biggest maybe of them all? "Maybe if she were taller, or maybe if he looked like your favorite MCM. Maybe if you were a capricorn like your best friend. Maybe, if all these maybes were a reality, you would get a shot at happiness."

We permit the prevalent voices of society to reflect these emotions. We channel those "you can do better, you can be better, or you deserve better" phrases and let them become the voices in our heads. And with that, we hit the repeat button just to end up right back where we started in the first place. There are so many people who go through this cycle of unhappiness without realizing there is no "thing," no person or place, that can give you genuine, lasting happiness. And this is because happiness is not from the outside. It is from within.

You cannot be hypnotized into a state of happiness. Temporary euphoria, perhaps, can work but there is no amount of finger snapping that can suddenly put you in a happy place. Even drugs cannot get you there. Certain drugs may loosen any emotional tethers that keep you in that dark tunnel, but they'll never truly set you free. If anything, this entangles things further, leaving you completely dependent on a drug for any form of reprieve, however temporary.

Stoicism takes you on a journey to self by eliminating destructive thoughts and behavioral patterns that you probably were not aware of. And the beauty of following the Stoic process is that the power is put back in your hands. Let me offer a quick illustration: Three ladies went out on a beautiful sunny day. Suddenly, the clouds darkened and a light rain began to fall. The first lady had anticipated this, and brought out her umbrella and a raincoat. Even her shoes were chosen for the weather. For her, the crisis was averted. The second lady made a poor attempt at shielding herself from the rain, all the while thinking about how her outfit and the entire day is ruined. In her case, the crisis was asserted.

Stoicism

The third person thought of her hair puffing up like a puffer fish if the rain touches it, and laughed at the image as she made a dash for cover. She might have gotten a little wet, but in her case, I would say, the crisis was diverted.

So, we have three different people who all had the same thing happen, but their experiences were different. The rain falls on everyone. Your status, your race, and not even your mind can stop the rain from falling on you. In the same way, life happens to everyone. It is your mindset that determines the experiences you will get out of life. Stoicism opens your mind, empowers you for life's journey, and puts you in a position to determine what your life's experiences will be—including how happy you are with your life.

Chapter Two
History of Stoicism

"If one does not know to which port one is sailing,

no wind is favorable."

Seneca

To understand Stoicism, it is important that we travel back in time to the era of revolutionary thinking. A time when the value of a man was determined by the soundness of his mind and the strength of his shield. Stoicism has its roots in Ancient Greece. A lot of experts believe the earliest voice of Stoicism was the great philosopher Socrates who, ironically, is said to have fathered the philosophy of Cynicism, as well. Both philosophies share some similarities, but there are a great many differences between the two. The true founding father of Stoicism is Zeno, who stumbled on the philosophical teachings of Socrates by accident—literally.

Before founding the Stoic school of philosophy, Zeno was a very successful merchant who traveled across the seas from his home town, in what we now know as Cyprus, to many places for trade. One of these places was Greece. On one of his many trips, he survived a shipwreck. Surviving something as terrifying as that puts people in a sober, contemplative state, and I think this was his state of mind when he decided to put aside his business plan and head for Athens. While Zeno was in Athens, he paid a visit to the city's library, and while he was there, he came across manuscripts discussing the great Socrates.

If you don't know who Socrates is, his teachings founded western philosophy. While he didn't do any writing himself, his most ardent students and disciples Plato and Xenophon documented his teachings. The manuscript that Zeno discovered was written by Xenophon, and Zeno loved the writer's portrayal of Socrates so much that he wanted to find and meet a man just like him. Zeno was discussing this with the person who'd sold him the manuscript when Crates of Thebes walked by. The bookseller directed Zeno to him.

Before we go further into the history of Stoicism, it is important to highlight the series of accidents that led Zeno to this point. First, there was the shipwreck. Next was his discovery of the manuscript written by Xenophon, and then, the fortuitous meeting with Crates of Thebes. It is said in one of Zeno's biographies that he famously joked, "Now that I have suffered shipwreck, I am on a good journey." In other versions, Zeno was quoted as saying, "You've done well, fortune, driving me thus to philosophy." This kind of thinking, converting the experiences of one's misfortune into a source of pure happiness, this is exactly what Stoicism is about. Now, back to the story.

Crates of Thebes was a well-known Cynic philosopher and, in his time, Cynicism was fairly popular (not widely practiced, but known) among the people. He was born to wealth but, based on his beliefs, Crates gave away everything he owned to live a life of poverty on the streets of Athens. He ate on the streets, slept on the streets, defecated on the streets, and was even known to have masturbated on the streets. As if this public way of life wasn't bad enough, he was said to be lame in one leg and he had hunched shoulders. So, he was an extreme Cynic who was somewhat disabled, but he was highly respected by the people of Athens. His allure to the people wasn't just because he nobly gave away his wealth for poverty, but the fact that in that bare and simple state, he lived a cheerful life.

One student of his put it this way: "But Crates with only his wallet and tattered cloak laughed out his life jocosely, as if he had been always at a festival."

So well-liked was Crates that people nicknamed him the "door opener," because he could enter any house and was received with honor

Stoicism

everywhere he went. He went on to attract a wealthy heiress who gave up her wealth, married him, and joined him in living on the streets. Hipparchia was known to have borne him at least two children. This was remarkable, because the idea of a woman—a high-born woman, at that—choosing to live in that way was abhorrent. But they did, and their marriage worked because of it.

Picture this chance meeting between Zeno and Crates. On one hand, you have this guy who just lost his wealth at sea and is now trying to make sense of his life, in a low emotional state. On the other hand, you have a guy who had all this wealth and looked like he would have been a lot more comfortable in his physical condition if he was wealthy, yet he willingly gave it away. To top it off, he was immensely happy. What an impression this would have made on our young Zeno!

Armed with the manuscript about Socrates, Zeno followed Crates and became an ardent student of his. However, Zeno did not entirely follow his teacher's ways. Zeno imbibed the idea of living a simple life but he believed in modesty, as well. I'm guessing the street life wasn't for Zeno. He studied under other philosophers of his time, too, but Crates had the greatest influence on him. Unlike his cheery and humorous teacher, though, Zeno was perceived to be gloomy and withdrawn.

He chose his company carefully and was not keen on making long, elaborate speeches. He was an earnest man of purpose, and even his death is reported to have reflected this. He was said to have died quoting a line from Niobe's tragic tale, "I come, I come, why dost thou call for me?" Everything had a purpose for Zeno, and this was emphasized in his teachings. He started his teachings in a place called Stoa Poikile, which is where the name "Stoic" originated from. At first, poets who originated from this area were called Stoic but, thanks to Zeno's influence, his followers and disciples were later known as Stoics.

Here was a man on the precipice of his greatest tragedy. He had lost a significant portion of his wealth on a voyage. While there has never been a time when being poor was easy, I believe people in this era likely had it even worse. Poverty was considered vulgar. People clung to their wealth like their lives depended on it. Their sense of purpose, sense of freedom, and sense of happiness were determined by the size of their wallets. We are not so far from this kind of thinking in today's world—the major difference is what we consider as wealth.

Stoicism

Back then, the quality of one's tunic was considered a marker for wealth. The number of fields you owned, and the number of laborers you had on it, were also signs. Even the number of children one had played a role defining one's social status. Today, we look at the number of cars you have. The pricier the model, the more points you earn. Our sense of accomplishment hangs on the number of likes and followers we are able to attract on social media. These are different concepts, but the context remains the same.

The early teachers of that time sought to help people remove the limitations placed on their happiness by wealth or the absence of it.

Chapter Three
Early Stoicism

"The purpose of life is happiness, which is achieved by virtue,

living according to the dictates of reason, ethical and philosophical

training, self-reflection, careful judgment and inner calm."
Stoic Quote

Given that Stoicism sort of descended from Cynicism, it is understandable that the early practitioners of Stoicism may have had to work harder to convince people that they are different from the Cynics. One famous poet, centuries after the death of Zeno, is reported to have jokingly said in one of his satires that the major difference between a Stoic and a Cynic was their choice of clothing. Given that Zeno was heavily influenced by one of the extreme Cynics of his time (Crates), you can't blame people for making this assumption.

However, true followers understood the clear difference. Zeno, in his teaching, broke down philosophy into three major areas—logic, physics, and ethics. He believed these three things were elemental to achieving complete peace of mind. Zeno was not a man of many words, but the founder of Stoicism wrote many articles on the subject of man's control over his mind and his wanton cravings. Sadly, none survived through time. We have fragments of his statements quoted by other writers, but it is his teachings and principles, as well as his vision for the Stoic society passed on to his students, that gives us his general view of life from a Stoic perspective.

Logic

On the subject of logic, Zeno believed there are four stages a person must go through before he can attain true knowledge. First came perception, or one's impression of a matter. The next stage is the person's acknowledgment of the matter, which Zeno referred to as assent. After acceptance, the next stage on this journey is comprehension. And it is only after the individual has gained full comprehension of the matter that he can really get true knowledge of it. Logic is a broad subject that covers not just the theories of perception and thought, but included rhetoric and grammar, as well. Zeno's thoughts on logic were influenced by one of his teachers at the Megarian school of philosophy in Attica, where he studied under great philosophers.

Now, while the teachings of Zeno started the Stoic movement in his time, certain prominent philosophers may have felt that his teachings, particularly on the subject of logic, were a somewhat watered-down version of what had been taught by some of his predecessors. One man who voiced this opinion was Marcus Tullius Cicero, a philosopher and lawyer who is considered to be Rome's greatest orator of the 1st century. But the life and times of Cicero happened long after the passing of Zeno, and he did very little for the Stoic community. However, Chrysippus, who later took over as head of the school of Stoic, had in hindsight protected the school from such attacks. We will get to him later.

Physics

In Stoic teachings, physics is more than the science of things. It explores nature in its rawest form and identifies the Universe as God. His view was not bestowing humane qualities on inanimate objects. He reasoned that the universe is the whole to which every other part belongs, and that the universe is a divine reasoning entity that advances and extends itself by creating. Zeno believed that universes undergo cycles of formation and destruction, a process which starts with the primary form of the universe—fire. From fire, it becomes air, which becomes part water and part earth. The water then becomes air again before going back to fire.

The interesting part of Zeno's early view on physics is that our souls are all part of the same fire, which is the primary substance of the universe. The differences in our thinking, our status as well as other physical attributes, is a result of the transformation process. At our core, though, we are all the same. And it goes on to tell us that the nature of the universe is balanced. It sets out to accomplish what is right. And, even though our actions and choices might take us on different paths and create alternate routes to our destination, Zeno recognizes the impact of unconditional fate in its design to keep the balance in the face of free will.

Ethics

The subject of ethics is where the early Stoics clearly distinguished themselves from the Cynics. The Cynics held the belief that if a thing is morally indifferent, it cannot be of any value. Therefore, since a house is just a thing to provide shelter, cannot be defined as being good or bad. Nearly all worldly possessions take on the same characteristic, which is why most Cynics disowned any wealth they had. Extremists like Crates lived their entire lives with nothing to their name. Another known Cynic extremist at that time is Diogenes of Sinope. He was said to beg for a living, and his home on the streets was in a ceramic jar.

Zeno, despite his great respect for Crates, did not necessarily agree with him in this regard. He was of the opinion that things that cater to our natural instinct for self-preservation could have some relative value apportioned to them. However, he made it ostentatiously clear that the value provided by these things does not in any way lead us to happiness. Zeno maintains in his teachings that happiness is directly dependent on our moral actions, and no moral action is more virtuous than the other. Our actions are either good or bad.

This kind of thinking resolves a lot of emotional conflicts that arise from the internal debate we have concerning the actions we take. This thought process is crucial to help weed out the unnecessary challenges we place upon ourselves. In a world where we are constantly seeking labels for ourselves, our thoughts, and virtually everything we do, the early Stoic life sought to connect us with the foundation of it all—our sense of reason. Zeno identified four negative emotions, and the three corresponding emotions to these four. Zeno was unable to find any corresponding rational equivalent emotion for pain. So, you have the positive "will" for the negative "desire," "caution" for "fear," and "joy" for "pleasure."

Desire and pleasure are words we don't identify as negative today. However, these are emotions that we typically confuse for joy in our quest for happiness. You desire a thing, seek it out, when you attain it, for a brief moment, you are "happy"—only to realize that this happiness is fleeting. And, because you want to retain this feeling of happiness, you divert your desires to something else and repeat the cycle. Zeno understood this and, even though his time is different from our time, the human interaction and emotional reaction to the world remains a static process. The early Stoics sought peace in their simple way of life while preserving the balance with their natural instincts.

Chapter Four
Modern Stoicism

"It is not what happens to you, but how you react to it that matters."
Epictetus

In the last chapter, we took a philosophical tour through the years 500 – 200 BC, and even touched on the first century to set the precipice for the beginning of Stoicism. We know the people, logic, and ideas that influenced Stoicism in its earliest years, and we also know that all of Zeno's works were lost. But, after the death of Zeno, how was stoicism able to persevere, evolve, and take root in society? And how relevant is the Stoic way of thinking in today's world? Well, the answer to that is simple—great ideas outlive the people and the times in which they were conceived. That said, in this chapter, we are retracing the Stoic movement after the passing of Zeno and following in the footsteps of his pupils and disciples to more conventional times. Now, I am certain that you came to this book for enlightenment, not a history lesson—but I should point out that sometimes, to get to where you want to go, you have to pay attention to where you have been (especially if you are lost).

Stoicism

And so, for a few more minutes, let us lose ourselves in the city of Athens. After Zeno's death, one of his most devout pupils, Cleanthes, took over leadership of the school. His story was just as tragic as that of Zeno's: He was a boxer of some repute in his early years, but when he came to Athens, he had barely enough money to feed himself for the day. He chose to study philosophy with the greats. First, with Crates the Cynic, but he soon took to Zeno. Cleanthes lived the Stoic life and was considered by many to be a man of character. He made valuable contributions to Stoicism, particularly in the area of physics.

Cleanthes elaborated on Zeno's notion about everything in the Universe being a part of one. He characterized the soul as a material substance, and claimed souls go on to live even after one's death. And on the subject of ethics, he emphasized the role our will has over our emotions. In other words, what Zeno started, Cleanthes completed—and he did this quite literally in some cases. For example, it is a general belief that Zeno was quoted as saying, "the goal of life is to live consistently," and Cleanthes was said to have added, "with nature." This completes the popular Stoic mantra, "the goal of life is to live consistently with nature."

The contributions of Cleanthes broadened Zeno's view of Stoicism but the real game changer came from Chryssipus. I mentioned him earlier, in passing, but now, we will look at his role in this story. Cleanthes may have broadened Zeno's theories, but it was Chryssipus who expounded on them, who crystalized Zeno's thoughts and set Stoicism on a path that influenced the minds of some of the greatest philosophers of the eras that followed, and even right down to this day.

His interpretation of Zeno's teachings did what in modern terminology would be described as setting the Stoic school on fire. For those who didn't grasp the teachings of Stoicism in the initial stages, this guy made it clearer. The practice spread across lands and transitioned into the lifestyles of many people in that time. This laid the foundation for the integration of Stoicism into cultures and religion, even though the people who adopted Stoic principles didn't identify as Stoics. This explains why we hear Stoic quips here and there. In this era, Stoicism transcended just being the "new age" religion of the time. Chryssipus laid out practical principles for daily living. He taught how to get to the root of emotional problems and provided a guideline to help extricate ourselves from the chains we have put on ourselves with our own expectations and ambitions. There were so many voices at that time, but Chryssipus created a cohesion for these different opinions, which probably explains why people accused him of quoting other philosophers in his writings.

His comprehension of the ideologies presented at the time made it possible for Stoicism to gain a definitive stand. His achievements and arguments earned Chryssipus recognition as one of the foremost logicians of Greece, and some even place him above Aristotle. Some proficient Stoics who benefited from his teachings and were recognized are:

Seneca

This is a wealthy poet and philosopher who is quoted throughout this book; he offered practical guides on living the Stoic life. Also, he is one of those Stoics who didn't disavow wealth—on the contrary, he was one of the wealthiest Stoics of his time. This tells us that Stoicism does not despise wealth, therefore embracing the Stoic life does not mean embracing poverty.

Epictetus

In contrast to Seneca, Epictetus was a slave who rose to the ranks of highly respected philosophers. He was born into slavery somewhere in Turkey and had a master who let him study. When he was given his freedom, he went on to teach philosophy. One of the people he influenced was Marcus Aurelius.

Marcus Aurelius

Seneca was known to have gained more wealth, power, and influence for being the tutor for the young lad who later became a much-disliked emperor, but Marcus Aurelius became powerful because he was an emperor and a staunch Stoic, as well. His reign was plagued with wars and troubles and, despite the tremendous power he wielded, Marcus was considered noble, just, and devoid of corruption—proving that a Stoic can have power and still be true to his beliefs.

Modern-day thought leaders who adopted Stoicism includes the likes of Theodore Roosevelt, Robert Louise Stevenson, and Bill Clinton. However, in the centuries that followed the reign of Marcus Aurelius, Stoicism was looked on publicly with contempt and it wasn't until the 20th century that it made a comeback. This return was thanks to the recognition given to Stoicism for its immense contribution to logic and other aspects of science, particularly mathematics.

Stoicism

But, we are not here to discuss the math, physics, and science of Stoicism. We are here to elevate our minds above circumstances in order to attain complete peace of mind. I wanted us to go on this historical journey for several reasons beyond helping us gain an understanding of the origin of Stoicism. I want us to look at the men who founded Stoicism. They were men limited by the science of their time. They were beaten down by life but, despite the tragedies they suffered, they shaped the outcome of their lives and influenced their world by elevating their minds. They didn't just say the words that we have come to appreciate: they lived those words.

Their journey to elevation started with the opening of their minds. And it is time for you to open your own mind. With history out of the way, let us examine the Stoic principles and logic.

Chapter Five
The Stoic Logic

"As long as you live, keep learning how to live."
Seneca

Stoic logic in textbook context is the system of formal logical reasoning that is concerned with the practical application of philosophy designed to help people live better lives daily. The Stoic logic covers every aspect of your life, from sex to emotions and even your social interactions with others. The concept of Stoicism is so encompassing that these principles still resonate deeply with us today, though they have been around since 400 years BC. The founders of Stoicism were so ahead of their time, the advancements made in modern-day technology in the areas of computer science, artificial intelligence, and many others are made possible largely due to the groundbreaking discoveries made by these Stoic philosophers.

More important than the machinery we have become so heavily reliant on is the impact of Stoicism on our lives. According to Stoic logic, when it comes to human behavior, everything we do is determined by our ability to reason. The Stoic logic is about embracing the power of decision making. The world we live in today has sold us on the idea of living off our desires. The bigger your house, the more fulfilled you will be. The more expensive the cars you drive, the more respected you will become. The wealthier you are, the happier you will feel. And so, we are trained to want more. We desire the latest phones, fashion items, and anything else the media sells to us based on the picture they have painted.

However, there is also a school of thought which, like the old school of Cynics, frowns on anything that could add value to your life. Under the guise of religion and beliefs, people are manipulated to discourage the seeking of wealth, power, knowledge, or anything that could put them in a position to be of any kind of influence. This kind of thinking limits them from achieving their true potential and making any kind of valuable contribution to the world. It also makes them more susceptible to the manipulation of others because, like it or not, we need these things to preserve our dignity.

On top of these conflicting views on life and our insatiable appetite for more "things," we are forced to deal with life. We know life is not going to be put on hold simply because you are trying to earn your degree, finish that project, or build that relationship. I watched a movie where the actor says life is like an endless series of train wrecks, with only brief commercial breaks of happiness. Not everyone goes through the same cycles of happiness interspersed with moments of grief. For some of us, the pain comes in short doses, while for others, the pain goes on for longer. And then, you have people who have dealt with pain all of their lives. No matter who you are, just as I mentioned earlier, the rain falls on us all.

People say the circumstances we go through in life shape us and make us better. That kind of thinking can work in certain situations, but what about events that cause senseless pain? In those moments of grief, you are unable to gain a proper understanding of why these things happened to you and how it is meant to make you better. If you are lucky enough, you are able to move forward with your life, but you may remain scarred by the experience. There will always be residues of the pain caused by the event. Those who are not so lucky may enter into emotional warfare that causes them to hurt themselves, as well as those around them. Their inability to make sense of their tragedy plunges them into depression and, until they get to the root of the problem, they will continue to relive this pain on a daily basis. The thinking that your circumstances shape you puts you at the disposal of life. You are left to the whims of these events, like being aboard a ship with no wheel and no captain to steer it—you will drift whichever way the storms toss you. If you are not careful, that ship could end up breaking apart.

The Stoic logic trains you to steer your ship with strength and conviction, even in the face of life's stormy waters. And if by chance the storms you face steer you in a direction you are not going, with wisdom and careful decisions, you can chart your course to take you to where you want to go, or even make a better life for yourself in the place you now find yourself. With the Stoic logic, even in the eye of the storm, you are in charge. Your decisions come from a place of rational thinking—when you are able to think rationally, the choices available to you become clearer.

The founders and major contributors to the advancement of Stoicism are people whose lives and teachings direct us on how to attain perfect peace of mind, even when we are going through hardships. The goal is to get to that place where you can live the good life. Now, what is the good life? We have established that wealth and the accumulation of stuff is not the good life. This can contribute to improving your quality of life, but even with the absence of these things, you can still live the good life. And that is because the good life is a state where we are living in agreement with nature. This definitely does not portend living in our basic state just like animals, because we have the one thing that animals do not possess—the ability to reason.

The good life for the Stoic is where all actions are a byproduct of the application of sound reasoning. It is easy to confuse a true Stoic with one who is obsessed with being in control, because they appear to linger on their thoughts and rarely take action without thinking it through. However, the decision to apply reason to their every action comes from a place where they recognize the things which they cannot control, and instead focus on what they can. With this perspective, you may find they are much more fluid, if not a direct opposite of the rigid impression we have of them. The fluidity of the Stoic allows them to go with the ebb and flow of life without necessarily being subject to it.

When the Stoic logic is narrowed down to the goal of living the good life, it does sound rather simple and uncomplicated, but you would be right in assuming that it is anything but. This is why there are guiding principles to take us through each moment of our lives. In subsequent chapters, you will often see the word "virtue"—this word plays a major role in the Stoic logic. "Virtues," in this context, refer to the things we aspire to be and become.

For those of us who are used to living on the edge between light and darkness—in other words, people who like to stir up a little trouble every now and then—the Stoic path might seem a bit daunting. You may be worried about becoming a goody-two-shoes. However, while you are expected to apply reason to every action, it doesn't mean your life has to be boring. There is plenty of room to have fun and, more importantly, there is plenty of room for you to be better.

Instead of living off cheesy one-liners, use Stoic logic to become the most authentic version of yourself, where there are no compromises in values and moral integrity.

Chapter Six
General Misconceptions About Stoicism

"All our knowledge begins with the senses, proceeds then to the understanding and ends with reason.

There is nothing higher than reason."

Immanuel Kant

In order to overturn your thinking system, which is critical if you want Stoic logic to be effective in helping you achieve the goals you have laid out, it is important to examine the most common preconceived notions people have about Stoic logic. I talked about a few earlier but here, we are going to be more specific. I will start with the more common ones and build up from there.

1. That Stoicism is too austere

I believe this opinion stemmed from the early years of Stoicism, which was a time when Cynicism was in vogue. The Cynic lifestyle was about renouncing any worldly possession and living a pious life. Although the early Stoic masters made a clear distinction in this regard, it has taken a while for their differentiation to catch on.

It is also quite possible that the absence of a flamboyant lifestyle, typical of most Stoics, may make it seem like they do not have fun or enjoy life. The truth of this is simple: Stoic logic teaches you not to place value on wealth and material things, hence, you are not easily moved by materialism. Rather, you appreciate the contributions made in your life, but this doesn't control your actions.

2. That Stoicism is a religious sect

Again, in the early years, Stoicism had a cult-like following, which probably instigated the idea that it was a religious sect. More than being a religion, however, it is a way of thinking and reasoning. Unlike religions, where you are required to embrace every facet, Stoicism allows you to take certain elements and apply them in a way you see fit.

In the application of Stoic logic, a deity does not dictate your dealings in life. What you eat, how you dress, as well as what you do is dictated by your sense of right and wrong. However, your perspective is not the only factor in the decision-making process. You also have to consider how your actions may affect your relationships with others.

3. That Stoicism means withdrawal from the world

To practice Stoicism, you do not have to quit your day job, sell your house, and take up residence in a hidden monastery. You are not required to contemplate the mysteries of the universe from the silence of a cave, and you most certainly do not need to take a vow of silence just so you can activate the voice of reasoning within.

There are many people, both past and present, who were actively involved in their communities and maintained a vibrant social life, yet were staunch Stoics or, at the very least, practiced Stoic principles. If you need to take some time off from the pressures of life, by all means do so. This is a primary human need. But do not ignore the other primary human need to connect, either. The key is balance.

4. Stoics are emotionless

This may fall under the purview of the first misconception on the list, but I had to separate this from austerity because of its importance to our everyday lives. The average human experiences a variety of emotions. Some of these emotions are very uplifting, while others are soul crushing. On the larger scheme of things, some of these emotions are our body's biological defense against threats to our person.

Choosing to live without these emotional experiences is the exact opposite of what Stoicism teaches. Grief helps you cope with loss, fear keeps you alert for danger, and even anger serves the purpose of strengthening you to protect yourself. The Stoic logic allows you to experience these emotions, but trains you to avoid letting them dictate your actions—even when you are in your most riled upstate, your actions will be guided by rational thought.

Sure, the average Stoic is not going to have a temper tantrum when the waiter mixes up his order. That doesn't mean he wasn't angered by it. He simply chooses to react in a manner that is more productive to the situation. So, if by any chance, you signed up for this because you were hoping to become an unfeeling human, you may need to rethink your options.

5. Stoicism is hard

I think this is more a millennial thing. We are so used to life at the push of a button that going through things that require a process might seem tedious. You want to go into your meditation corner, connect your thumb to your finger, take a deep breath, and exhale all your troubles away.

Stoicism does not work that way. This is a lifelong process. Each day is lived with a conscientious effort to be mindful of everything we do. If you are hoping to correct certain behaviors, build your confidence, and live the good life, you will have to get used to the idea of applying Stoic logic every single day.

6. The practice of Stoicism removes your free will

The Stoic logic embraces the role fate plays in our lives. This essentially means you have to accept your place and station in life. Most people have interpreted this to mean that we are expected to simply roll over and play dead in the face of circumstances—this could not be more wrong.

The Stoic logic advocates people analyze their situation objectively. In the process of analyzing whatever is going on, they are able to truly understand what is in their control and what isn't. This kind of thinking puts them in harmony with the situation, because they have gained insight into the true nature of what they face. And it is with this knowledge that they can

Stoicism

take actions that will bring about the most desirable results.

Chapter Seven
Stoicism in Everyday Living

"When you arise in the morning, think of what a precious privilege it is to be alive –

to breathe, to think, to love, to enjoy."

Marcus Aurelius

Practicing Stoicism in modern times is not so different from being a Christian, a Buddhist, or practicing whatever customs and beliefs are prevalent in your community. It is not a religion, however, it is a way of life. Practitioners simply reflect on the teachings, then try as much as possible to engage their minds with topics and thoughts that offer better choices for their lives. Stoics are more proactive about their day-to-day living—they do not go to bed, wake up, and wait for life to happen to them as they go about their activities for the day. Instead, they do their best to anticipate the challenges of the day and plot corresponding actions to those challenges.

They meditate on the four cardinal virtues of fortitude, justice, temperance, and prudence, and try to envision how they may have to employ each of these virtues that day. This is not to say that they can predict the events of the day. However, they are able to program themselves to better handle the surprises life will have in store for them. The "programming" of the Stoic mind is done by participating in different Stoic exercises, which may include picturing a worst-case scenario for the day. Here, the Stoic thinks about the worst event that could happen that day, then build their mindset to be indifferent towards this tragedy. This exercise is called Hierocles' circle.

This does not necessarily mean that the Stoic wants this tragedy to happen. Obviously, we would rather have good things happen to us. But this kind of training puts your mind in a state where you are able to remove your sense of value and self-worth from the event. If you are like most people, your biggest fear would be the loss of your source of livelihood. With the standard mindset, a loss like that could lead to depression, panic, and other negative emotions that may instigate negative reactions. This exercise helps you eliminate that fear. So, even if it happens, you are able to live above this crisis.

For some people, this kind of thinking may appear morbid, especially if your worst fear is your own death. Often, these fears stop us from living our day-to-day lives. I know of a woman who barely escaped her marriage by the skin of her teeth, due to her abusive husband. With help from friends and family, she was able to bring him to justice and have him sent to jail. It was a temporary victory for her, because his sentencing became a countdown clock that caused her to experience anxiety and panic attacks.

She would jump out of her sleep in a state of fright, thinking that day would be the day her husband would walk free. She couldn't take on jobs, was scared to buy a house, and couldn't even enjoy a simple moment with family because at any moment, her ex-husband might walk through her door. She practiced the Hierocles circle exercise. In those moments of meditation, she dug up every horrible version of her nightmare. Where she was dragged by her hair on the streets, where he murdered her in her sleep—it was gory and, in the initial stages, it was discombobulating.

But she kept at it. In her own words, the visions became less frightening over time until she found herself trying to invent scarier scenarios to amp up the fright level. However, the truth was, she had lived out her worst fears and this opened up a new door for her. She signed up for self-defense classes, not because she wanted to fight but because it helped her feel more confident. She moved closer to her family and opened up more to her friends. The paralysis imposed by fear ceased the moment she overcame her fears.

Stoicism

This is just one example of how Stoicism can be applied in your life.

Another relevant benefit of the practice of Stoicism is its ability to help you focus on the present. There is so much going on around us in life—so many passions, so many dreams, so many opportunities and, in the same vein, so many fears. The uncertainty of tomorrow is what drives a lot of us on a fundamental level. The prospect of paying those heavy, recurring bills have us sitting at our desks day after day, working jobs we have no interest in. We settle for relationships that cause us more harm than good, because we are afraid of being lonely.

In situations where we are meant to speak up for our rights, we allow our fears to silence us—but more than anything, we spend our days worrying. We worry about what could have been, what should have been, and what would have been. Some of us worry more about the past. Previous mistakes and actions taken haunt us and prevent us from enjoying what is happening now. Then, you have people who are the exact opposite—they live in the moment, but for the wrong reasons.

These are the people who live only for their desires and passions. They must buy that new fall coat. They must own the latest phone. If everyone is doing it, it must be okay for them to do it, too. It's like pulling beads along a string that has no end. They just keep picking one bead after the other. Never experiencing happiness, never truly enjoying the moment. All they do is want more. This is the bane of living in these modern times. The practice of Stoicism can keep you grounded in the present. Seneca put it this way:

"The greatest blessings of mankind are within us and within our reach. A wise man is content with his lot, whatever it may be, without wishing for what he has not."

You do not need to embrace Stoicism in its entirety. You can take up Stoic exercises that you feel would bring you closer to your goals. Throughout the rest of the chapters, I will share some of these exercises and offer guides to help you integrate them into your daily routine.

Chapter Eight
The Four Cardinal Virtues of Stoicism

"Everything we hear is an opinion, not a fact. Everything we see is a perspective, not the truth."

Marcus Aurelius

You cannot practice Stoicism without first understanding its cardinal virtues. The origin of these virtues is unclear, but they predate the earliest Stoic teachings. Perhaps going even further back than the time of Plato. If you look on the internet, you may find different variations of the words typically used as the four cardinals. This is because of the difficulty in translating ancient Greek texts to the English language. There is also the conflict of perspective. The only philosophical dictionary known to have survived from the ancient Greek times come from Plato's era, which means the definition is given from a Platonist perspective. Unfortunately, there are no definitions from the Stoic era.

However, given the materials we do have, we are able to gain a better understanding of what the Stoics thought. We will look at each virtue individually:

Phronêsis: Prudence or Practical Wisdom

This is the most important of the Stoic virtues and it refers to our ability to discern good from bad. It is believed that wisdom is the only virtue, while the remaining three cardinal virtues which we will discuss shortly are simply its primary applications. Seeing that wisdom is essentially practical reasoning, I tend to agree with that thinking.

Wisdom is the foundation of all Stoic logic, because you cannot make sound decisions and actions if you have no clear understanding of what is good and what is bad. In this application, good does not refer to what appeals to the senses. The smell of a nice, warm bowl of soup can be very appealing to whoever perceives it, but that does not automatically ascribe the moral value of good to it. The bowl of soup falls under the preferred indifferent category. Eating this bowl of soup will not make you a good person or a terrible person, it is how you go about your pursuit of the soup—whether you steal it or cook it—that is classified as either good or bad.

Wisdom is the understanding of the true nature of good. With this understanding, you are able to ascribe value to different external things rationally. Under Stoic teachings, a wise person is not just someone who can tell the difference between good and bad. For a person to call himself wise, he must be able to offer himself wise counsel. In other words, wisdom is an internalized process.

Dikaiosunê: Justice or Morality

Again, this is an area where we have issues with the direct translation of the word. When you hear justice, you may think this refers to the legal sense of the word, but that definition is simply not enough to encapsulate the true Stoic reference of this virtue. While an aspect of this virtue implies a state where we are obedient to the laws of the land, it goes much deeper than this.

Morality, on the other hand, does not fully encompass the stoic meaning of the word, either. In this instance, we are talking about doing right or, as some people would like to say, living an upright life. If you are the religious sort, you may go as far as calling it righteousness. However, between morality and justice, we can understand what this virtue is about.

In practical terms, justice or morality is the application of wisdom in social interactions. We've established that wisdom is the knowledge of good and bad, and the ability to clearly distinguish between both. It is one thing to know something, it is another thing to act on it. In your dealings with people, justice/morality refers to the wisdom you apply in relating to them. Your respect and treatment of others is not based on their status, gender, or the benefits they offer. Rather, you make a deliberate choice to be fair and impartial.

Sôphrosunê: Temperance or Moderation

In some books, this is referred to as self-discipline or self-control. In life, we are almost always in a constant state of want. And, more often than not, our wants are not always the same as our needs. Our carnality is propelled by what books like the Bible refer to as the "desires of the flesh."

The entire sales force in the world is built on this concept. You turn on the TV to see a nice-looking guy running and, without so many words, you are programmed to think that to get that body, you need to run—and for your running to feel good, you need the shoes he is wearing. This prompting of your desire is so strong that even if you have 10 sports shoes lined up in the back of your closet, you still feel you need this one shoe.

This kind of feeling is amplified in areas of our lives that have to do with gratifying our pleasure impulses. This virtue is all about tempering those instincts that drive our wants. It is, in essence, the application of wisdom when dealing with temptations.

Andreia: Fortitude or Courage

Fear is another prominent driving emotion behind most of our decisions. You find people who work themselves to the bones because they are afraid of not being able to afford the things they want. They sometimes live a stagnant and unprogressive life, deliberately avoiding risks that would propel them forward, even if those risks are supported by their rational thinking or wisdom.

This virtue grants the ability to act on the wisdom you have discerned, even if it is not exactly conventional. Wisdom is fantastic, but without the application of wisdom, it is just another nice thing something thought or said. This virtue is also likened to endurance. But in that sad, long-suffering way that makes you a victim of circumstance. But in an emboldened form that sees you facing down your deepest fears and not acting on them. Rather, you push past it to think and act logically. You can say fortitude is wisdom applied in adversity.

Chapter Nine
The Practice of Misfortune

"Say to yourself in the early morning:
I shall meet today ungrateful, violent,
treacherous, envious, uncharitable men.
All of these things have come upon them
through ignorance of real good and ill...
I can neither be harmed by any of them,
for no man will involve me in wrong,
nor can I be angry with my kinsman or hate him;
for we have come into the world to work together."

Marcus Aurelius

Optimism is good. Hope is good. Maintaining a positive outlook on life is good. These are vital tools in the world we live in today. But if you want to thrive, if you really want to live the good life and you have found yourself struggling with this, perhaps it is time to throw away the rose-tinted glasses and step into the dark for a minute. For people who have characterized themselves by their ability to maintain a sunny-side-up attitude toward life, looking on the flip side might be likened to them violating their nature, but hear me out.

Stoicism

For a long time, we have been taught to believe in concepts like luck, grace, supernatural blessings, and so on. While some may deny the existence of these things, it would be detrimental to live our lives hoping that one of them (if not all of them) happens to us. The reality is that life is more like a game of chess—it requires strategy and careful planning. To develop and execute a well-thought-out strategy, you need to see the picture from all angles, anticipating the best- and the worst-case scenarios. This may sound morbid, but stay with me.

The "hashtag blessed" movement that is so rampant on social media, as well as in our regular daily lives, is not what it appears to be. That person who seemingly got lucky went through a process you are not entirely aware of. In Stoicism, there is a generally held belief that luck is simply preparation meeting opportunity. Except in most cases, these "lucky" people get into their favored season without any deliberate preparation on their part. Stoics don't stumble into their season. They prepare themselves adequately and, when the right moment comes, they seize it. But how do you prepare for something that is not exactly within your control?

For starters, you have to stop thinking you are just someone life happens to. Obviously, it would be delusional to think you have any form of control over the universe. Remember that boat on the sea illustration I used earlier. There is no way you can dictate the direction of the wind or the movement of the waves, and certainly not the intensity of the storm. However, that doesn't mean that every time your ship is tossed, you lose your position as captain. The wheel is still in your hands—you just need to activate your thinking hat. Here are a few things you can start doing:

1. Get out of your comfort zone.

The general saying, "if it's broke, don't fix it," is a lie that feeds the delusion many of us call "optimism." The reality of life is the constancy of change. If you do not determine the change that will definitely come, the change that comes will determine your fate.

2. Expect the worst but hope for the best.

We have this habit of making decisions based on the best-case scenario while living in fear of the worst. This is the source of anxiety and fear. Instead, develop the habit of taking actions based on your worst fears, living on the hope that the best will happen. This is not to say your fear should guide your actions. The Stoic exercises we will talk about later will clarify this.

3. Be deliberate in your efforts

Each day should not be just another series of meaningless routines. Break patterns, but don't be impulsive about it. Think it through and ensure that at the end of your thinking process, you are able to conclusively establish actions that support what you have discerned.

STOIC EXERCISES THAT HELP IN THE PRACTICE OF MISFORTUNE

1. PRACTICE POVERTY

I can almost picture that one eyebrow shooting up to your hairline as you read this. I mean, after everything I did to convince you that Stoicism is not a vow of poverty, the very first Stoic exercise I share is to tell you to practice poverty. It sounds insane, but in a minute, it will make sense. Comfort is a form of slavery, because it conditions your happiness to the things you have. A loss of those things would result in a major disruption of your life. More than that, it would affect your emotions negatively and cause you to react in the same way. The amount of suicides recorded during America's great financial depression illustrates this.

The practice of poverty involves taking a few days each month to live conservatively, well below your means. During this period, you would eat very little, and ignore that comfy bed to sleep on the cold, hard ground. If you can, dress in your rattiest clothes. Essentially, you should familiarize yourself with being in a state of want. The benefits of this exercise are that it keeps you in touch with reality and helps you get to a place where you can appreciate the things that give you comfort without depending on them as a source of happiness. By so doing, you are able to see those "things" for what they really are. Whether it is your job, your home, or your wealth, the goal is to be able to enjoy them—not be enslaved by them.

2. PRACTICE WHAT YOU FEAR

As humans, it is instinctive to want to get as far away as possible from the thing you fear. Our need to distance ourselves from our fears is so intense that, sometimes, it drives us to the point of denial. We refuse to acknowledge the threat, and the price we pay for this denial can be very high. On the other end of the spectrum, you have people who go to extreme lengths to avoid what they fear most. Either way, we are deprived of

Stoicism

living to our fullest potential, because we are being held down by our fears.

I know of someone who came from a family where breast cancer was prevalent. This was the time when the management of cancer did not include some of the medical advancements being made today. This meant there were a lot of deaths from cancer within the family, which led to the women and some of the men living in fear. For the longest time, this woman lived in the shadow of the disease. She bought into the slogan of "living in the moment," but in the worst possible way—she spent money as fast as she could earn it, and rarely made plans beyond the next week.

On the surface, she seemed to be living the life. She was fun, energetic, and a joy to be around. But in her heart, her fears ate away at her. She turned down jobs, marriage proposals, and basically any opportunity that held any future prospects. By chance, she was involved in an accident that almost took her life. Lying in pain in her hospital bed forced her to confront her fear—she realized cancer was not the only thing that could kill her. So, right there, she decided to get screened. She figured if she can survive that accident, she can survive cancer. That's how she became free from her fears.

3. PARCH YOUR IGNORANCE

Have you ever asked yourself why you are afraid in the first place? I have an intense phobia of snakes. I am usually described as calm and collected, and I'm able to maintain this ambiance even under the most intense high-pressure situation. But throw in a slippery, slimy snake, and I lose my cool in the most embarrassing way imaginable. My reaction was unexplainable. It felt like it was something I was programmed to do. One evening, I was watching a documentary, listening to this explorer talk about snakes and his mission to ensure the survival of a certain species. I was stunned that anyone cared enough to do this. But the more I listened, the more I realized that, in their way, snakes are beautiful, too. And yes, a fraction of them are poisonous, but through the eyes of this explorer, I could see their beauty.

My fear of snakes was based on the stereotypical information I was fed all my life. But the moment I replaced that ignorance with factual knowledge, my fear reduced a significant degree. Don't get anything twisted, though—there's no chance of me having a snake as a pet in the nearest future, and I still think that the way they move is super creepy. Still, I'm not as terrified as I once was.

Stoicism

In this exercise, you need to dry up the well of ignorance that feeds your fear by asking the right questions. For example, you might have a fear of losing your job, because of the downsizing rumor you heard. Have a talk with your colleagues and go over your performance to help determine if your fears are valid. Then, ask the tough questions. Is it the loss of a paycheck or the prospect of finding a new job that scares you? The answers you get will give you the confidence to face the future and, most importantly, it demystifies your fear. Because the truth is, the thing that really scares us is not necessarily the thing or event itself, but rather our mind's often exaggerated interpretation of it.

Chapter Ten
The Training of Perception

"You act like mortals in all that you fear,
and like immortals in all that you desire."

Lucius Annaeus Seneca

Anyone who knows me knows I am a big fan of wildlife documentaries. Of course, if given a choice, I would choose my concrete jungle any day, but that is neither here nor there. The point is, wildlife fascinates me. This is how I found out something very interesting about the way lions hunt in the wild—and it is nothing like what we were shown in *The Lion King*.

When lions hunt, whether in a pack or solo, they stalk their prey. They have a selection process for this prey, which could be based on a number of factors like the desirability of the prey, its vulnerability, and so on. And when the lion sets their sights on prey, they keep their focus on it until they sense that the timing is right. Then, they lunge an attack. If this attack occurs where the selected prey is in the midst of other prey, a stampede occurs as the other animals try to get away from the lion.

In the midst of the chaos, you'll see hooves flying left and right, but the lion keeps its focus on the prey it has selected. If you examine clips of these attacks, you will find that in the middle of the chase, other prey likely could have made it to the lion's dinner plate with very little effort, but because they are not the selected prey, the lions miss out on that opportunity. This scenario plays out in our lives, too. We have the things that we desire, and we often pursue those things with a single-minded focus. In pursuit of our goals, many of us develop a tunnel vision, which makes it impossible to see anything except the thing we most desire. And because of this, we tend to miss out on even better opportunities—just like the lion.

This kind of behavior is also prevalent in our relationships. The world has more than seven billion people living in it, and still, we have millions of people who are experiencing loneliness to the point of depression. This is not because of the absence of people in their environment, it is their perception of people that puts up a barrier preventing genuine relationships from forming. To live the good life, it is important to train yourself to see things from the right perspective. When I say the "right" perspective, I'm not referring to good vs. bad—I am simply talking about a view of life that allows you to harness and maximize opportunities and relationships.

This kind of thinking can be applied to our emotions, as well. Today, we live in a world where it feels like everyone is overly sensitive about everything. In modern colloquialism, people are easily triggered. A parent enforcing discipline can easily be interpreted as a form of violation or the abuse of the child's rights. Your decision to support your personal beliefs can be seen as an act of discrimination. And often, we are on the receiving end of that stick. We see ourselves as victims—and sometimes we are—so everything we hear can seem to be a direct attack on our person or our way of life. Social media has become a platform that amplifies voices, whether it is your own voice or the voices of others. And, given the amount of time we dedicate to these platforms, it is not surprising that it seems as though we are constantly in a triggered state.

But, like the Stoic virtue of wisdom teaches us, it is our duty to discern between good and bad and to understand the true nature of things. This can only be done if we train ourselves to see things a little differently. Perception is the force behind creativity. With the right kind of perception, you can create an experience that uplifts and inspires joy, regardless of the negative circumstances surrounding it. Marcus Aurelius put it perfectly:

Stoicism

> ***"Choose not to be harmed and you won't be harmed. Don't feel harmed and you haven't been."***

I have outlined a few Stoic exercises you can apply daily to help you train your perception.

1. TURN THE OBSTACLE UPSIDE DOWN

This is an exercise that aims to turn a negative experience into a source of good. It works by taking something you can describe as a huge thorn in your side and looking at how it can become a blessing to you. When I thought of an illustration for this, what came to mind as parents. If you are a parent to a strong-willed child, you understand what it is like to be at your wit's end, where you are on the verge of pulling the hair off your head because you are can't get them to do something as simple as taking a bath. It can be a frustrating experience—or, it can be an opportunity to learn and apply patience. Your crazy boss at work could be a chance to learn people management skills, and your misery at work could present a way for you to find out what makes you happy.

2. CLARIFY YOUR THOUGHTS

Unless you have been living under a rock most of your life, chances are many voices shaped the way you think. The first voices were those of your family, but you also have your friends and peers from school, as well as your teachers who used the books (the voices of others) to impact you. And let us not forget your experiences in life. All these things allow you to look at the external structure of an apple and decide if it is healthy and good enough to eat. However, we also apply these things to our dealings with people, as well as our experiences in life. This serves us to an extent, but it can also become limiting as you develop preconceived notions of how things should be, how people should behave, and so on. Your narrow-minded perspective limits you from enjoying people or moments. To clarify your thoughts, take time every day to isolate yourself from the world. Cast aside any personal opinions you have about people and examine the facts of the situation. This gives you pure insight, untainted by any bias. With this perception, you can alter the reality of your situation.

Chapter Eleven
Keeping the Balance with Eupatheiai

"The happiness of your life depends on the quality of your thoughts."

Marcus Aurelius

If you have never wanted something so badly it affects your ability to sleep at night, I am not sure if I should congratulate you or feel sorry for you. But my thoughts on the matter are beside the point—I simply wanted to draw your attention to the intensity of our passions and how far they can drive us. There is a distinct difference between passion and desire, although we often use them interchangeably. Desire has more to do with your wants, while passions are more of a need. Desires have a more sedentary effect, while passions have been known to start global wars. Why am I talking about this, you may wonder?

he Stoic life, as I established earlier, is not a life devoid of passions. It is my personal belief that it is impossible to be impassionate and stoic at the same, because Stoicism is about being true to your nature and, as humans, we are created to be passionate. Stoicism teaches you to control your passions, and the only way to stay passionate about life without letting your passions control you is to find balance. In the previous chapter, we talked about training your perspective, and this has a lot of great mental benefits. One of them is helping you attain a balanced insight. In a general sense, the exercises discussed herein are helpful, but if your problem is deeper than that, you need exercises that are more focused.

The Greek word for passion describes passion as emotions that are irrational, excessive, and mostly unhealthy. One common example of emotions that may fall in this category is anger. We all experience anger at some point, whether it occurs as mild irritation or a consuming rage. The intensity of your anger is dependent on how triggered you are by the event that brought it on in the first place. The real distinguishing factor is how we react to the anger triggered in us. Some have a passive-aggressive reaction while others may choose to ignore the incident with the hope the anger will go away. But anger never really goes away if you don't deal with it; it just recedes to the background where it continues to build up like the countdown timer of a bomb until, one day, there is an explosive display of rage.

A historical example of reacting to anger in extremity is the story of Alexander the Great, who killed one of his closest friends in a fit of rage. He immediately regretted his actions and was so consumed by grief, he could not eat or sleep for three days. You may not have gone to this extreme to express your rage, but without control, you could do something you will later regret. Emotions like jealousy and greed can also have a devastating effect. The Greeks called all of these passions "pathetic." To control your pathetic, you have to replace them with eupatheiai, which are the exact opposite. A good example of an emotion that can be classified as eupatheiai is joy. Seeing as we cannot surgically remove those negative emotions and replace them with happy ones, there are Stoic exercises you can do to curb your impulses and, in the very least, slow down your reactions. If you find yourself struggling with anger, envy, and depression, there is a strong possibility that your ability to be rational has been compromised. Your mind, in this state, is teetering toward thoughts that promote self-agenda, therefore you are likely to be unbalanced. To level the scales, try the following exercises:

1. Remind yourself that everything is temporary

Nothing in life lasts forever, and this applies to the things that make us emotional in an unhealthy way. Go back to your early teenage years, when you felt that if you did not attend that much talked-about party, you would die. Your parents stood their ground and you didn't attend but guess what? You didn't die. And I can bet that if you had the chance to attend that party as your current self, you would find it pretty lame. My point is, right now, the thing troubling you may seem overwhelming, but in a few days, months, or years, it won't even matter. It doesn't make sense to take actions that could have a lasting effect for something that is ephemeral. Always remind yourself that this, too, will pass.

2. Remember that you are small

Sometimes, our wealth and status in life fool us into thinking we are incredibly important. The world's inability to treat everyone equally fuels this foolery. You may find men and women who are so obviously beautiful, they think their very existence is a favor to the rest of the world. As pride sets in, they may begin to treat people in horrible ways. But the truth is, in the grand scheme of things, we are such a tiny speck that neither our presence nor absence affects life. You may be so wealthy that you have many people whose livelihood depends on you, but you would be terribly mistaken if you think that the moment you walk out of their lives, they would stop living. Anger is sometimes a by-product of pride. Remember the infinitesimal role you play, and you might be able to keep those unhealthy emotions in check.

3. Let history be your teacher

This time, I am not talking about your history—I am referring to the history of great men and women who came before you. Their greatest achievements, as well as their biggest failures, could help you nurture your ambition and, at the same time, humble it. But never use history to justify your actions. If your goals are driving you to the point of unhealthy obsession, a history lesson might be the thing you need to help keep your ambition alive without compromising your values. History is like a kind of mirror and if you look closely, you might find your reflection in the lives of those who came before you. But it also exposes a glaring truth—the actions of people are what outlive them. Egypt had beautiful architectural buildings during its time, but no one remembers who built them. Time can make you obsolete, regardless of your achievements.

4. Be aware that death comes to all

We have established that everything is temporary. All those nice things you want so passionately have an expiry date. Even if you are able to obtain them, ownership of that thing is temporary. Even the life you live can't last forever. So, when you feel yourself slipping into that space where your ambition is overpowering your virtue, pondering on the fact that death is the final end for everything may help you keep your emotions in check. By reflecting on these truths, you able to gradually subdue your patheiai and open the door for your eupatheiai to reign.

Chapter Twelve
Plato's View

"If one has made a mistake and fails to correct it,

one has made an even greater mistake."

Plato

Plato, as you know, was one of the greats. His teachings were studied by early Stoics and even though they disagreed with him on certain things, his works laid a good foundation for some Stoic principles. For the sake of this chapter, we will focus on Plato's view on idealism. Idealism is an aspect of philosophy where reality is asserted as we know it through our own mental construct. In other words, we create our own reality. The word in itself was born from the Greek word *idein,* which means "to see." In broader terms, idealism is meant to represent the world as it might be or as it should be. Don't mistake it for optimism, which is essentially hope in the future success of something. Idealism acknowledges the present state of things, but takes actions based on what the situation has the potential to become.

With this established, let us bring things back to our real-life situation. I am going to use our relationships to illustrate this. We typically have a firm idea of how we would like each relationship in our lives to play out. These relationship ideals are what form the basis for our expectations. We want our partners, friends, family, and even perfect strangers to think, act, and behave in a certain way. Having ideals and expectations for relationships are good, but if these ideals are drawn from the wrong place, you are simply setting up yourself up for failure. Let's talk about romance.

For years, Hollywood and romantic writers have told us what love is meant to be. Ladies want to be swept off their feet, and men have been programmed to look for that damsel in distress. We all enter into relationships with these expectations. But then, reality shows us a different side of things. Men are so busy trying to be providers that they have very little time to attend to the emotional needs of their partners. The only thing they are on the lookout for is an obvious sign of distress, which would prompt them to step in and show off their manliness. Women, on the other hand, are no longer waiting to be rescued—they have become much stronger. While there are now fewer scenarios where they are in distress, their emotional needs remain very high. Not a lot of men recognize this, so you often find women who are emotionally unfulfilled in their relationships.

Stoicism

The ideals fed to us by Hollywood make it difficult to pay attention to the things that really matter, like how our partners resolve conflict, how they handle rejection, and the quality of our communication. Instead, we focus on sex, material gifts, and everything else glamorized by the movies we love. So, when we meet prospective partners, we see them through rose-colored glasses that make them appear perfect. Our instincts may warn us of certain things that seem off, but we typically prefer to cling to that idea of perfection rather than face the problem at hand. It is like a woman walking into a designer store to buy a nice pair of size 12 red shoes, but leaving with a size 8 green pair and hoping that by the time she gets home, it will magically transform into what she really wants. This sounds ridiculous, but this is what we do in most of our relationships.

The Stoic approach to resolving this is to first draw your ideals from the right place. There are many books and resources that talk about relationships and offer tips on escaping the hurdles most couples will encounter. They may sound like the right place to draw your relationship ideals from; however, you must remember one crucial fact. Every relationship has its own DNA. Any resource you find on the subject can only offer a single perspective, so you need to go somewhere that gives you a bird's eye view of things. And one person that really teaches us to do this is Plato (and now you know why I mentioned him in the beginning).

Plato's view is referred to as the view from above because when you channel it correctly, you are able to see everything at once. This helps reorient your judgment of people. It also humbles your assessment of the situation, which is very handy if you are the type of person who hears a hello from a prospective partner and immediately starts hearing wedding bells. Identify your priorities in a relationship with this Stoic exercise that help get that bird's eye view:

Try to see everything at once

This is tricky, as we have a tendency to be short-sighted. Even though you have trained yourself to think long term, your objectives may be your own self-preservation. And, on the universal scale of things, that kind of thinking in itself is short-sighted. To see everything at once is to look at things from every angle that you can explore. When Marcus Aurelius described Plato's view, he put it this way:

"Whenever you want to talk about people, it's best to take the bird's eye view and see everything at once – of gatherings, armies,

farms, weddings and divorces, births and deaths, noisy courtrooms and silent spaces, every foreign people, holidays, memorials, markets – all blended together and arranged in a pairing of opposites."

The world, they say, is now a global village and to an extent, this is true. But seeing the world through these "lenses" narrows our perspective on life. Say, for instance, you are dealing with the negative opinions of others. We give credit to these voices and limit our potentials to these criticisms because we feel these opinions are important.

Take a moment to silence the voices and think of the boisterous life going on around you. The endless chatter, the cycle of life, the simple mundane activities of people—do these negative opinions influence or affect life in the tiniest bit? No. Sure, the words might hurt, but they are like paper planes thrown at a rock. They can only make an impact if you amplify the sound. This overhead view gives you a perspective that reveals the grandness of the universe and downplays the illusion of people's individual roles within it. Essentially, other people's opinions aren't really that important.

Chapter Thirteen
Memento Mori (Remember Death)

"It is not death that a man should fear, but he should fear never beginning to live."
Stoic Quote

One of the Stoic exercises I talked about earlier had to do with remembering that death comes to everyone. Memento Mori aims to take that concept a step further. More than just being a symbol for change, this seeks to initiate reflection of one's own mortality. I once read a relationship book that brought readers deeper into the recesses of the male mind. The goal of the book, essentially, was to help women understand how men work, and to use that information to manipulate men into giving them what they want. Many of the things discussed in the book are things I would agree with, to an extent, but I am also of the opinion that while those things may be true, they are not right.

One topic that stood out was the idea that a man's worth is determined by his job. In other words, if a man loves his job, it's likely this man would love himself, and vice versa. My disagreement is the fact that we ascribe this quality to a specific gender. This is a generation and a time when a person's worth is determined by the substance they possess, regardless of gender. That is not to say that this kind of thinking started today; in fact, this has been prevalent throughout the ages. Preferential treatment is given to those who have more. If you are at the receiving end of this preferential treatment, it is easy for this power to go to your head.

I can see you sitting on your chair and judging some political figure for doing exactly this but, you see, the fingers point back at you—this abuse of power is not limited to the elite. We perpetuate this behavior in our corners of the world, as well. How have you behaved since you got that promotion at work? Have you taken advantage of your position at the expense of others? There is a reason they say, "power corrupts, and absolute power corrupts absolutely." In the same way they say, "money amplifies the character of a man." So, if you had an issue with ego when you were barely getting by financially, coming into wealth is only going to make that character flaw even more noticeable. When we get this kind of power, we start to feel invincible. We start thinking we are exempted from the law and that certain things don't apply to us. This is very dangerous, because you may start acting recklessly. And when you are reckless, you are at risk of self-destructing. This is why when seemingly normal people land a position of power or wealth, they just "lose" it.

However, it is critical that I mention here that neither wealth nor power is evil nor good. This is a Stoic perspective, and no one illustrates this better than Marcus Aurelius himself. This man was one of the most powerful men in an empire that was considered one of the most powerful in the world at the time. The kind of power he wielded can only be described as that absolute power, which is famous for corrupting those who possess it. Yet Marcus was humble, fair in all of his dealings and a man of true strength of character. Proving that it is possible to be powerful, wealthy, and still be a force for incredible good. And, while it may sound like I am talking about some fantastical character straight out of a Marvel comic, I assure you there are regular people like that in our day-to-day lives and no, they were not born that way—it requires immense self-discipline on a daily basis. The exercises we talked about can help you in the area of curbing excessive unhealthy behavior, but if you find yourself making reckless decisions that endanger you and those around you, or perhaps your ego is competing with the universe, you need a healthy dose of humility.

Stoicism

In Stoicism, for every virtue we seek, there is a corresponding vice that you need to uproot. The objective is to replace vice with virtue. Now, you and I started this journey because you want to live the good life. We have defined what the good life is from a Stoic perspective. One crucial element of this life is maintaining harmony with the universe. I did this quick trip back to the beginning to bring us into focus, because humility is something many of us struggle with. I have heard people question the purpose of humility. We think it is a quality that keeps us in the gutter with people we consider undesirables. But without humility, you may never be able to get out of your comfort zone. For too long, we have identified fear as the primary reason many of us want to stay where we are, and yes, fear can hold us back. But ego is what makes you stagnant. When you start to think you know it all, you have it all, you create chains that anchor you to that spot in life. To break those chains, spend your mornings meditating on scenes guided by the following thought processes:

1. See your death vividly

I read about a group of early Stoics who would occasionally hold a feast in the presence of a corpse. This is insane, just as the thought of seeing your death, but only if you are missing the point. And the point here is to find the answer to this question. How big is your ego going to be when you are six feet under? Nobody looks at a corpse and marvels at its intelligence or how wealthy it was. The best quality that can be attributed to a corpse is that it looks "restful," and not even the artistic skills of the best mortician can change this. Despite the commonly-held belief in an afterlife, your influence over the living ceases the day you die. The effect of death on the body of a rich, influential person is exactly the same on that of a poor nobody. Death, which is the conclusive end of all things, pays no attention to things that make you think that you are better than everyone. Instead of pondering on those superficial things that feed your ego, meditate on your death and recognize that, in the end, none of those things matter—everyone meets the same end.

2. Acknowledge that tomorrow is not guaranteed

If you are one of those people who loves to procrastinate, meditating on this could help you be more proactive. If you are also struggling with your relationships, this meditation exercise can help bring things into perspective. We have a tendency to take things for granted. We abuse the grace of waking up to see each day. We don't appreciate those in our lives, because we take their presence for granted. What would you regret the most if you died right now? If you can do something about it now, do it and stop putting it off. Tell those you care about how much you appreciate them.

Chapter Fourteen
Recognizing Limits

"Life is like a play: it's not the length, but the excellence of the acting that matters."
Seneca

The serenity prayer was written sometime in the 30s and has become a very important mantra for anyone seeking to correct certain behavioral patterns. And while it has Christian origins (the original version was written by a theologian), it does have a lot in common with something Epictetus wrote in his time. If you are not familiar with the serenity prayer, here it is:

"God, grant me the serenity to accept the things I cannot change,

Courage to change the things I can,

And wisdom to know the difference."

Epictetus, on the other hand, wrote:

"Make the best use of what is in your power, and take the rest of it as it happens. Some things are up to us and some things are not up to us. Our opinions are up to us, and our impulses, desires, aversions—in short, whatever is our

doing. Our bodies are not up to us, nor are our possessions, our reputations, or our public offices, or, that is, whatever is not our doing."

The words are different, but the implied meaning is the same—despite the fact that one was written a few centuries BC. It is a high-pressure world we live in. The pedestal for success is really high and because success is obscenely celebrated, we feel even more pressure to achieve more. For every industry, there is a standard and, sadly, these standards are mostly unrealistic and unattainable—still, that does not stop us from reaching for those things. Beauty, for instance, is now defined by having high prominent cheekbones, thick pouty lips, and perfectly arched eyebrows. We see these beautiful models in magazines and on television, and use them as a yardstick to define our beauty.

I think it is either we chose to be ignorant or we simply do not pay attention to the fact that these so-called beauties attained that perfection with the help of a makeup artist who has artfully sculpted the face of the model with the tools at her disposal. And, in the areas where the skills of the makeup artist fall short, professional photographers used light and shadows to play up the model's best features. And where the photographer was unable to attain perfection, there was the graphic artist who used technology to airbrush out any flaws. In other words, what we have adopted as the yardstick for beauty is the product of a group of people whose goal is to sell a product to you. Except that you end up buying both the product and their concept of beauty.

The same process applies to body image. We buy into an unrealistic idea of perfection and almost kill ourselves, literally, to attain it. As kids, we were programmed to go to school, get good grades, graduate at the top of our class, and take on high-paying jobs to cater to a high-profile lifestyle. As if that was not stressful enough, you still have to make time to have the perfect love life, get married, and create that ideal home where the kids are well-behaved around the clock and your partner adores you 24 hours a day. Failure to attain any of these activates conditions like depression, poor self-esteem, and a general negative outlook on life.

The reality is, going into life with perfection as your expectation is setting yourself up for disappointment. There is no such thing as perfect. While there may be moments that are perfect, they are just a fragment in time. If you spend your days obsessing over the things you want to happen, you will miss out on those glorious perfect moments, and your life may seem like a series of sad events—even when you succeed in certain areas, your victory would taste like ashes in your mouth because you cannot get over your emotions long enough to appreciate and celebrate your feats.

This exercise helps you shed the burden of these stressors so you can connect with what is really important. By recognizing what lies within your control, you are able to productively channel your energy and resources into activities that will significantly improve the quality of your life.

1. Be naked with yourself

I mean this literally and figuratively. When was the last time you stood in front of a full-length mirror to look at yourself? Stand naked without any shape-wear, makeup, or wigs. Don't suck in your tummy, tilt your head for a better angle, or try to cover up any flaws. In Stoicism, we are taught to accept ourselves as we are. You may buy into the general logic that justifies our personal discrimination against ourselves with the need to become a better versions of you. However, this logic fails to deliver any value if you are unable to appreciate yourself as you are. While your body may not match up to the current dictates for the perfect body, you still have a lot of things to appreciate about the body you have. As you do this exercise, you also have to remind yourself that trends fade. For women, there was a time when the skinny body was the rave of the moment, and that transitioned into the era that directed their perfection lenses to the more voluptuous body type. You have to try to not take trends too seriously, because your body is going to serve you for the rest of your natural life.

2. Ask the right questions

Stress has received a lot of bad press for being the harbinger of heart diseases, blood pressure problems, and myriad other chronic illnesses. Stress has been known to stem from our physical, emotional, or mental participation in activities that take us outside our comfort zone. While stepping out your comfort zone is essential for growth, the transition process is not always easy. When you find yourself in highly stressful situations, take a step back and ask yourself, what do I have control over? What can I actually do about the situation, and should I really do it? The answers may help you determine what is up to you and keep you from obsessing over what isn't.

Chapter Fifteen
Journaling

"Leisure without books is death, and burial of a man alive."

Lucius Annaeus Seneca

We have all heard this at some point. As a child, I used to view this exercise as the most important way to deal with my emotions. As I grew older, read more, and generally attained more knowledge, I have come to see journaling as one of the most effective non-confrontational ways to deal with emotions. I arrived at this conclusion long before I became aware of the great Stoics who, as it turns out, agree. Before I go any further explaining how this plays out in our lives and what Stoic teachers had to say, I would like to dispel the notion that journaling is a feminine thing. Many of us assume journaling to be a "dear diary" moment, and Hollywood's biggest ode to masculine journaling is the *Diary of a Wimpy Kid* which doesn't do much to remove the gender stigma attached to it. In reality, strong historical figures like Albert Einstein, Charles Darwin, Leonardo da Vinci, and Thomas Edison were known to keep journals. So, do not let the idea that journaling may be emasculating stand in your way.

In Stoicism, you are expected to start the day by visualizing the outcome (for me, this is one of the coolest Stoic exercises), and end the day reflecting on everything that has happened. It may sound nice to just sit down with a nice glass of wine and go over the events of the day, but if you really want to do the whole deliberate living thing—which is what Stoicism is about—you are going to need to whip out a pen and a notebook and start writing. I appreciate that some of us have the memory of an elephant and can remember even the most minute details, but journaling helps you gain a broader view on things. But that is not the only benefit of journaling:

1. It provides an outlet for your emotions

One of my childhood friends who struggled with anger was able to control her outbursts and improve her relationships with others through journaling. Whenever she felt triggered, rather than lash out—which was her typical reaction whenever she felt this way—she opted to pour all of her feelings into her journaling. At first, it was like a painted board of raw emotions. But as she evolved, she realized that she started writing more constructive descriptions of her emotions, which gave her a more objective view of the situation. Her anger never disappeared entirely, but she was able to react less aggressively.

2. It helps promote self-awareness

Certain things about yourself will come to light when you start journaling, and it may surprise you. For instance, there might be situations that upset you that you have been struggling to deal with. But because you are dealing with the symptoms and not the root cause of the problem, nothing appears to be working. And, most times, you are unaware of this. Journaling connects you with your inner-most thoughts and, while the whole picture may not show up with just one night of journaling, you will get the answers you need with consistency.

3. It helps push you towards your goal

Nothing makes your vision clearer than writing it down. When you have all these things you want to do and achieve but life keeps throwing hurdles and challenges, it can end up distracting you if you are not focused. Writing down your goals gives you clarity of purpose, and when you have a strong sense of purpose, you are able to strategize effectively towards achieving them.

I could write a whole book on the benefits of journaling, but it makes sense to stick with these for the purpose of this book. Writing a journal is just one half of the equation—reading it is the other. To enjoy the full benefits of journaling, you have to imbibe the habit of both writing and reading what you wrote. It can be a bit tedious, seeing as you are the author and you certainly know what you put in your journal. However, the objective of this exercise is to gain a deeper insight into what you do and why you do it. To help you get maximum benefits from this, here are a few things you can do:

1. Pick a subject to write on

You have the freedom to write about anything that is going on in your life, but you gain more from the experience if you narrow down the subject. You could start with your thoughts and hopes for the day, and how you intend to go about achieving your daily goals. Or, you could decide to write about your last emotional incident. Talk about your reactions and why you think you reacted that way.

2. Use your words

Your journal doesn't have to compete with the latest bestseller on the market. You don't need to fill it with an impressive lineup of hard to pronounce words just so to seem smart to the reader (which most likely is only you). This is an intimate moment with yourself, and does not need to be embellished. All you need is honesty. This is another opportunity to be naked with yourself. Use the words you are most comfortable with, and just let them come to you. Also, don't worry if you are barely filling out a page the first few times. That, too, will come with time.

3. Don't read to criticize your work

Chances are you are going to find a lot of cringe-worthy moments when you go through your journal. Perhaps it was the way you reacted to something, or some previous misconception you had about a person or situation. Either way, you are going to find some not so proud moments. Embrace those flaws and view them as an opportunity to grow and be better. That said, obsessing over a few "I's" you forgot to dot and the "t's" you forgot to cross is a total waste of time. Save that attitude for school projects or communications with employers and clients.

4. Chose specific times for journaling

If you are the type of person who is able to concentrate in the middle of chaos, kudos to you. For the most part, journaling requires quiet time and space where you are able to spend time alone with your thoughts and feelings. But the right time is dependent on what you want to achieve. For instance, you might journal at the start or end of the day if you want to be consistent in pursuing your goals. If you journal when you feel emotionally triggered, your objective is to exercise control over your reactions.

Chapter Sixteen
Premeditatio Malorum (The Premeditation of Evil)

"We should every night call ourselves to an account;

What infirmity have I mastered today?

What passions opposed? What temptation resisted?

What virtue acquired?

Our vices will abort of themselves if they be brought every day to the shrift."

Lucius Annaeus Seneca

This is another one of those exercises that might sound morbid or creepy when you take it at face value: You are expected to anticipate the very things you are subconsciously hoping will never happen to you. I can even understand why, even though people respected the early Stoics, they were more comfortable keeping them away from their homes. But if you sit down and consider this topic for a minute, it starts making a lot of sense. The good life is about having a healthy balance. Keeping your focus on only the positives instead of planning for what you have tagged as the "bad stuff" makes you ill-prepared for those situations, which often eventually come whether we want it or not. Granted, it never fully plays out the way we envisioned it, but it happens nevertheless.

One truth of life we are never willing to accept is that bad things happen to us even when we have worked hard to earn the good things of life. In fact, I cannot think of any person (with a heart) who would walk up to someone experiencing a tragedy and say they deserved what they are getting—even if the person facing those hard times is incredibly cruel and generally disliked, we still do not wish the worst on them. If we feel this way about people we do not like, it is easy to imagine how we would feel about ourselves and those we love, especially when our self-preservation instincts set in. And, if I am being honest, there is nothing wrong with wanting the best for yourself—but you would be doing yourself a great disservice if you do not brace yourself for the worst.

If the name of the exercise bothers you, instead of calling it the premeditation of evil, think of it as a safety drill. Almost every public building in any civilized society has a safety drill, which usually consists of a series or sequence of routines that are meant to be executed in the event of an incident that threatens the safety of the building or the people in it. For these safety routines to be developed and perfected, the people who set it up had to anticipate something terrible that could compromise safety. That is not to say that they were actively hoping for terrible things to happen. In fact, you can see they are going out of their way to make sure that tragedy does not happen. But they recognize that a change to the safety status of the building is inevitable, and rather than twiddle their thumbs, they put safety measures in place. Often, they will even go further to get the personnel to reenact potential threatening situations and then play out a routine that would keep everyone safe.

This is what this exercise is about. We already know that the only constant in life is change. So, even if we live in this fortified bubble that makes us feel safe and cocooned away from anything that might harm us, the wise thing is to appreciate what we have been blessed with while preparing for the event that might take all those things away. Now, just because you are anticipating the negative things does not mean you should go into full apocalypse mode. For as long as mankind has existed, we have always lived in fear of that gloomy day when the whole world would be consumed in one swoop. Some say it will be some sort of natural disaster of huge proportions. Others say it will be a religious phenomenon separating the good from the bad. While the world has had its fair share of natural disasters, it has survived through the ages. In essence, this should not be your worry. Life's hurricane affect each of us individually, at different phases in our lives.

Seneca has this to say about premeditating evils:

"Nothing happens to the wise man against his expectation… nor do all things turn out for him as he wished but as he reckoned—and, above all, he reckoned that something could block his plans.
"

What he is saying, in essence, is that this exercise helps you prepare for anything that might disrupt your plans, while helping you figure out how to use those disruptions in your plans to your advantage. So, whether you make a loss or a gain, you are well prepared for it. How exactly do you go about this exercise?

1. Rehearse your day

Start your day by visualizing every aspect of it. Think of what would happen to your loved ones if you suddenly suffered a tragedy. Would they be taken care of? Let's say you have a presentation to make at work. What would happen if there was a glitch with the computer system—how would you be able to deliver excellently, despite the setback? What if the client doesn't like what is being pitched? Do you have a backup plan? Go over every important event that might occur throughout your day.

2. Practice being calm

In the face of calamity, we tend to lose our wits, but expending our energies this way is an unproductive waste of time—this does nothing to change the situation. Part of this exercise aims to help you come to terms with the alternate realities of your circumstance. While it is not guaranteed that those things will come to pass, you should still prepare for them emotionally, mentally, and physically. Face down your fears by accepting these possible realities and plan accordingly.

3. Take action

Wallowing in thoughts of what might or might not happen after you have made your projections is unwise. Instead, make concrete plans and create a "safety drill" of your own that factors in the contingencies you have put in place, just in case some things don't go the way you have planned. However, keep Seneca's quote at the back of your mind. Even with your exquisite and well-thought-out backup plan, things may not play out exactly as you wish—but your visualizations make you better prepared for the unexpected.

Chapter Seventeen
Amor Fati (Love Fate)

"Accept the things to which fate binds you, and love the people with whom fate brings you together,

but do so with all your heart."

Marcus Aurelius

Fate is a dangerous concept. The idea that certain events in our lives are predestined to happen is something we all struggle with. It makes us feel powerless in our bid to change the events that dictate our daily experience, and even when we come to a place of acceptance, we do so with dejection, sadness, and a "why me" attitude. Now, when I am talking about fate, I am not referring to what you had for breakfast—no, you were not fated to eat cereal this morning. Things like breakfast are within your control because you had a choice in the matter. A diagnosis of something you dreadful that you least expected, that is fate. Winning the powerball lottery on your first attempt also involves the hand of fate. Basically, anything that happens to you without your choice in the matter is fate. Although there are exceptions, fate does not need your permission.

James W. Williams

In line with today's double-standard custom, we tend to celebrate fate when it favors us. We don't question the abundant blessings we receive, even when we know we did not do anything to earn or deserve it. The moment things go awry, however, we get upset. These ill-fated setbacks drive us into an emotional downward spiral that we may never truly recover from. Many of us have made several attempts to fight fate. This rebellion sets us on a path that clearly has no end, yet we totally commit ourselves to it in the hope that, somehow, we can thwart fate. After wasting so much time and energy, we come to a place where we finally give in and surrender—except more often than not, we come to this realization a little too late, or after we have wasted so much time and resources trying to avoid what should have been embraced from the beginning.

Now, I'm not saying you should roll over and play dead when something you did not predict happens to you or the people you love. That would be ridiculous advice. But a scene from a very popular medical TV series often comes to my mind when I think of fate, and I believe that this is the best illustration for the point I am trying to make.

In this scene, there was a single dad who came to the hospital with his terminally ill daughter. This ailment was diagnosed from the time that this child was a baby and they had been managing her care ever since. However, the child suffered a major health crisis in this scene and according to the doctors, there was nothing else that could be medically done to improve things for her. In fact, they did not think she would make it through the night. The concerned dad understandably refused to accept the damning verdict. Instead, he raced out, leaving his daughter in the care of physicians while he made a mad dash to spring for a cure. He was out of money, out of time, and out of ideas, but he was willing to try anything that could offer the possibility of saving his young daughter's life. Naturally, it was heartbreaking. For a parent, it is instinctive to want to protect your child and he just followed his instinct, but in doing so, he nearly missed out on a moment he would never have been able to forgive himself for missing. So, if this moment was important to him, why was he out there fighting it? Because he did not embrace fate.

We are groomed to expect miracles, and while miracles are known to happen, they also fall within the realm of things we do not control. You cannot manipulate a miracle, just like you cannot manipulate fate. But in embracing fate, you don't take on the dormant role, even though it may feel like it. The reality is, your acceptance actually empowers you. Marcus Aurelius put it this way:

"A blazing fire makes flames and brightness out of everything that is thrown into it."

The fire is your potential. Obstacles, challenges, and fate's whims are the things that are thrown into the fire. Your decision not to embrace these things will not stop them from happening to you. As a matter of fact, you might see the embers of your potential burning out faster because you are unable to bring yourself to a place of acceptance. Seneca, who was a slave, a cripple, and later became one of the most influential men in Rome, put it this way:

"Do not seek for things to happen the way you want them to; rather, wish that what happens happen the way it happens; then you will be happy."

I have a few mental exercises that will help awaken a mindset within you that embraces this Stoic philosophy:

1. Be balanced in your thinking

When things happen to you, good or bad, train yourself not to react emotionally. While your instincts may be self-serving, they don't always serve a higher good. Think rationally and objectively, and let your actions be guided by this. During your thinking process, assess the situation by weighing in on the dangers and risks that threaten your objective. Ask the right questions that would provide solutions to those risks you listed out, then act accordingly.

2. Get comfortable with being uncomfortable

Since you have accepted that you cannot change what has happened, ask yourself how you can make it work to your advantage. This exercise is particularly good for people who have suffered some kind of trauma. Tragic as it was, it has already happened. There is no going back, no undoing, and certainly no forgetting. But you have a choice: accept it and redefine your experience, or fight it and let it control your experience. You've heard the expression, "If life gives you lemons, make lemonade." This just means to make the best of your situation. I remember losing a close friend of mine and, yes, his death was painful. I was racked with grief and couldn't function for days. But as I reflected on his life, I came to the realization that I could either celebrate his life—which was glorious—or wallow in his death. I chose life, and even though it still hurts to not have him here, I can find joy in the knowledge that I was privileged to know this amazing person.

Chapter Eighteen
The Power to Enforce Change

"It is the power of the mind to be unconquerable."

Seneca

If you read the Christian bible, you'll be familiar with the one story that strikes me as a modern Stoic. This happened during one of the teachings of Christ, who was generally disliked by the Pharisees and Sadducees—essentially the spiritual and philosophical thought leaders of their time. But Jesus was not necessarily afraid of them and his words explained why the son of a carpenter stood fearless in the face of their threats, anger, and accusations. To paraphrase, he admonished his followers not to be afraid of the person who can harm them physically; instead, they should fear the one who can harm their souls. This is a not a religious book, but I draw inspiration from great thought leaders and, in his time, Jesus was one of them. What he said was absolutely powerful and empowering at the same time.

The mind is the singular most powerful weapon mankind possesses. It is not your ability to wear the finest robes that separates you from primates. It is not your muscle that makes you more powerful than a full-grown lion, which is known to be a strong and fierce predator. It is your mind. If you groom it right and feed it right, it can put you in an untouchable position in life. It is not as though life doesn't happen to you. On the contrary—when your mind is being exercised the Stoic way, it would appear that you experience life even more than the average person. Your mind is the key to unlocking the true powers of the universe and, most importantly, the process of opening your mind is in your hand. Our concept of universal power fluctuates between Pinky's [from *Pinky and The Brain*] comical attempt at following his master's orders in their bid for world domination, and the eternal intergalactic battles between humans and other species. I don't blame people for thinking this way; I blame Hollywood. According to Stoic teachings, we are all a part of the universe and attaining universal power simply means you dominating your own corner. And when I say dominate, I am not referring to the fleet of cars in your garage or the exquisite private jet sitting in your hangar, or even the mansions you own on every continent. All those things are nice to have, but it is possible to own all these things and still not live the good life, much less dominate your universe.

Generally, life is very hard, even for those who seem to have everything they need to deal with its complications. Applying the principles of Stoicism helps you work with the tough hand life deals us on a daily basis. The most puzzling thing for me when I first came across the concept of Stoicism was the fact that, on paper, it sounds so simple. I mean, all you are expected to do is sit in your house and think about things, and then let the rest happen. But when it comes to application, it is a very complicated process. I think the most challenging thing for anyone is the fact that you have to unearth and discard patterns of behavioral and thinking processes that have been entrenched in you for decades. You have been taught to expect and plan for the good things in life. We know that we don't want bad stuff to happen, so we don't plan for it at all. Then, you have this principle telling you to sit down and think of everything that could go wrong before the sun goes down—and not only that, you are expected to plan for those things.

Every single Stoic principle is something that goes against the grain of our upbringing, and this is why it is going to be an uphill task. You are going to have to work extra hard to push the heavy barrel of your mind to the top of that hill. It is an extremely hard battle, but it is also a very rewarding experience when you are able to get yourself to the top. However, the battle does not end when you get there—it is only when you reach the top that you realize there are more hills for you to climb and, in true Stoic tradition, you cannot afford to get too comfortable with the hill that you have just conquered. You are going to have to roll up your sleeves and take on the new challenge. With each new hilltop you reach, you make an advancement in your life.

Another thing I find particularly fascinating about the Stoic teachings is that your experience, your process, and your journey is a personal one. Even if you are married with kids and have a huge, close-knit extended family, Stoicism is a lonely road. That barrel-up-the-hill process is one you take alone. You can draw insight from other people, just as we have drawn from the great Stoic philosophers I mentioned in this book. You can inspire others the same way others have inspired you, but no matter how close you are to a person, this is something you experience solo.

For people who have never ventured out into anything on their own, this can be a scary process, but power is not something to be afraid of. Especially since this is not the kind of power you wield over people, but over your experiences in life. If you have struggled with confidence issues, it is likely you have let the voices of others control your thoughts and actions for so long that your own has been put on permanent mute. You know how you feel, and perhaps what you want, but the voices of other people in your head automatically disqualify you, so you timidly sit back and let life just do its thing. By recognizing the truth—that these voices don't matter and that their opinions do not control the outcome for you—it is possible to block them out and gradually empower yours which, in truth, is the only relevant voice for your journey.

You can draw strength by echoing the words of thought leaders who support your goals but, at the end of the day, it is your voice that will help your mind create the experience you want. In the same way, if you have dealt with loss, you can find joy in the realization that death is not the finality of life. If you change your perception and see things from Plato's perspective, your mind can convert that experience into one that births a new beginning for you, and as many people as you would want to be affected by it. The founder of Alcoholics Anonymous turned his struggle with addiction into a program that has impacted and continues to impact the lives of millions globally. This is the power of your mind.

Chapter Nineteen
Stoicism in Cognitive Behavioral Therapy

"If you really want to escape the things that harass you,

what you are needing is not to be in a different place,

but to be a different person."

Lucius Annaeus Seneca

Sometimes, the depths we have sunk to in life make us pray fervently for a clean slate to help us start over. The truth is, even if you are given a clean slate, without truly addressing the problems at hand, you would likely end up creating the exact same messes you are trying to run from. The issue, then, is not the slate that we are praying for, but ourselves: the things we do, the things we say, and the way we act—these are the main problems that need to be fixed. Unfortunately, we do not have a reset button we can press when we start experiencing glitches, and then just get back with the program. But if you think about it, it really is not unfortunate such a button does not exist. If Thomas Edison had pressed the reset button after every one of his scientific failures, he would never have been able to become the inventor we recognize and respect today. He told us of his many failed experiments, but we don't remember him for that. In fact, his errors helped him upgrade his experiments. In the same way, the mistakes you make as a result of your behavioral tendencies don't necessarily define you. And, like Edison, you can upgrade. In a few minutes, you will find out how.

Cognitive behavioral therapy, or CBT, basically involves making a conscious decision and a deliberate effort to correct certain behaviors that are having a negative impact on your life and slowing down your performance in the area of achievement. CBT is not restricted to specific behavioral patterns—just isolate the patterns you want to replace and apply the Stoic principles. Before we get into the nitty-gritty of this, you should know that this is something that will require deliberate efforts on your part. Stoicism is generally discussed as philosophy, but it has a very strong therapeutic effect because it focuses on reframing the mind. Epictetus was said to state that, "the philosopher's school is the doctor's clinic." The teachings of Stoicism have both a preventative and proactive approach in CBT, and at the core of this is emotional resilience training—key in replacing bad behaviors with good practices. Rather than simply responding to instincts and reacting to emotions, you are taught to take a step back, evaluate your emotions and, most importantly, gain a better perspective of the situation.

There are three core areas that need to be influenced by Stoicism in order to set you on the path that effectively helps you correct your behaviors, and that is exactly what we are going to explore in the chapter. These core areas are your thoughts, your will, and your actions. Pay attention to each of these, because it is almost impossible to make any genuine progress if you are experiencing a setback in one aspect. Take what you learn here and apply it with wisdom.

YOUR THOUGHTS

They say that out of the abundance of the heart, the mouth speaks. In other words, what you say is a byproduct of what you have been thinking. The same thing goes for your actions. Your thoughts control your view of the world and how you perceive the people around you, and it is from the seat of your thoughts that your interpretations of life's experiences are transmitted. The things you do are dictated by what you think. For instance, if you find yourself reacting in anger every time someone uses a certain word or phrase, that reaction is simply a projection of your thoughts on that word or phrase. If you react to emotional crisis by overeating, it is because you have convinced yourself that the food helps.

The foundation of Stoic principles involves replacing vice with virtue, and this applies to what you think about, as well. Then, you need to consider how you think. Many of us make the mistake of thinking after we have taken action, and this impacts our behavior. To set your thoughts on the right path:

1. Feed your mind with materials that promote positive thinking. If you must read something that contains negative elements that could compromise your emotions, be objective in your assessment of it.

2. Ask questions. Just because things have always been done a certain way doesn't mean this is the right way. Take Plato's view of the situation: see everything from all angles and make your assessment from this perspective.

3. Manage your thoughts effectively. With so many things fighting for our attention, it is easy to get distracted. Use a journal to help you stay focused on your thoughts. Journaling also helps you isolate problematic thoughts that fuel negative energies.

YOUR ACTIONS

In our default setting, we react more than we act. Certain reactions are instinctive, but some are habits we have established over a long period of time. If you were ever physically abused, you may feel defensive if someone enters your physical space. This is an instinctive reaction. To correct instinctive behaviors, you have to start laying the psychological foundation, first. Start by getting to the root of the problem—in this case, deal with your vulnerability to let other people in.

To correct habitual behaviors, you need to make a deliberate decision to implement actionable steps. For instance, if you find yourself sleeping for less than four hours each night, you need to look at the things you do that take away from your sleep time. Things like your phone habits, bedtime routines, and even diet could play a role. When you have found out what is hindering your sleep, take the necessary steps to correct it. The key here is to act out your plans and make observations as you go along.

In order to effectively change the way you do things, you must do the following:

1. Think it through

You should not wake up one morning, snap your fingers, and decide you are going to change the way you do things. Often, you end up crashing out or losing interest long before you achieve your goals. Say, for instance, you want to lose weight. Don't just jump on the nearest treadmill or sign up for the first diet program you get your hands on. Think a little deeper. Why do you want to lose weight? Want kind of weight loss program is suitable for your lifestyle? These questions will help you get started on the right action plan.

2. Have a clear vision

It doesn't matter how noble your intentions are—without a vision, you are most likely going to get distracted or worse, fumble your way through the dark in a bid to reach your goals. Get a journal and write out what you hope to achieve with your actions. This helps you monitor your activities and can also serve as a source of inspiration that will motivate you and push you towards your goal. Remember, in order to change your habits, you have to be more deliberate about the actions you take.

3. Be consistent

To create sustainable lifelong habits that are beneficial to you and those around you, you are going to have to be consistent. The best athletes in the world carry out a routine series of activities on a daily basis. This training can be brutal for the average man, but for the athlete, excellence requires sacrifices, and sacrifice demands commitment. You cannot do something today, then ignore it and come back to it in the hopes that you can hit your goals. Stoicism does not work that way, and if you really want to use it as part of your CBT training, you need to discipline yourself to be consistent and persistent.

YOUR WILL

You have your actions on one end of the spectrum and your thoughts on the other. Your will is like the mediator between the two. For your thoughts to be translated into actions, you need your will. There are times when you may feel you cannot go any further, or that your goals are no longer worth the sacrifices you have to make to get to there. It is your will that will keep you in the game, so to speak. Your level of consistency and your ability to remain persistent even when you don't feel like it can be attributed to your willpower.

Wanting or wishing to do something is very different from having the willpower to actually do it. To muscle up your willpower, I would

Stoicism

recommend practicing the Stoic exercise of training your perspective. Flip the script by viewing the obstacles that threaten your ability to go through with the process as an opportunity to transform yourself. When athletes compete, they are confronted by opponents who appear stronger and more physically suited for the challenge as well as those who look weaker and less likely to win. But you don't see them back out of the race simply because they worry that their counterparts could defeat them. And, at the same time, they don't get cocky because they think they are better than their opponents. They simply enter the game with a focus on their own performance.

In the same way, when you step into the field of life, you have to keep your focus on yourself. When the negative thoughts and physical challenges come to distract you, stop fighting it off or giving in to your fears. Instead, see this as the opportunity that it really is and use it to fire up your ambition to be better.

Chapter Twenty
Stoicism in Pain Management

"He who is brave is free."
Seneca

Anyone who tells you that pain is just a state of mind should be smacked in the head—or better still, sent to a labor ward to watch a woman give birth to a child. Pain is a reaction to physical, mental, or emotional hurt. And it is a perfectly natural process. However, with the implementation of Stoic principles, you can control the intensity of the pain you feel, as well as the extent of the damage it may cause. It is a very difficult concept to accept, but it is not as foreign as we think. We have heard stories of brilliant people who work with intelligence agencies and are trained to withstand the most gruesome forms of torture without breaking. People who work in the military, air force, or navy are rumored to undergo similar pain management training in the event of their capture. Now, we are not going all gung ho on this like people who work with government security agencies, but there are some kinds of pain that do need to be managed.

For this topic, I will be discussing the two major types of pain that we experience: emotional pain and physical pain. In my opinion, all pain stems from these two types of pain, and if you can equip yourself to deal with it, you are in a better position to deal with all of the other stuff. But before we get into it, there is something you need to bear in mind. Pain is not your enemy. Don't make it your mission to seek out ways to numb yourself. There is a reason your body and mind were built with pain receptors. They can help you recognize your limits. Without those pain receptors, you run the risk of hurting yourself beyond repair. Without pain, you lose the ability to function like a normal human being. In a world that glorifies superheroes, we may aspire for a life where we live beyond the reach of pain. But if you look closely, you will see that your favorite heroes hurt, too. They do not live beyond pain; they have simply learned to live above it. Embrace your pain, and when you do, you will reclaim the power it has over you.

PHYSICAL PAIN

Don't let anyone tell you that the pain you are feeling is all in your head. We all experience pain at different levels. My six could be your two and your 10 could be someone else's five. This is not something to get into a competition over. It is just one of those realities that you are going to have to embrace. That said, there are several techniques that can be used to manage physical pain without relying on medication. These practices date back millennia. Women employed these techniques to help them cope with the pains of labor. Obviously, women have a lot of pain relief options for this now, but in the past, all they had was a cloth to chomp on and some mind games to get them through it. I am not even going to try and compare the pains of a woman in labor to anything, because I have been told that unless you are going through it, you are not going to understand it. Instead, I will use a more relatable kind of pain. And I found that in one of the greatest emperor that Rome had ever known: Marcus Aurelius.

Now, here was a man who suffered from chronic stomach ulcers, which prevented him from eating certain foods and eating at certain times. He was also known to experience chest pains and had issues sleeping. It is hard to accurately diagnose what Marcus was going through, but suffice it to say that he was in an incredible amount of pain, which he lived with for most of his life. His resilience has been attributed to his Stoic training. In a few short steps, you can build your own mental resilience towards pain.

1. Don't judge the pain

We have a tendency to identify pain as bad, but when you do that, you develop a knee-jerk response to it that can distress you even more. So, step one is to step off the judgment box. As I pointed out earlier, pain is not your enemy. Neither is it your friend. Detach your judgment of the pain from the experience of it.

2. Change your perspective

Pain does not really harm you in the stoic sense, as it does not hurt your morals. What affects you, though, is how you react to it—and wallowing in pain is considered a negative reaction. So, if it is not truly harming you in the areas that matter, can it really hurt you? The answer is no—not unless you let it. In other words, pain requires your permission to truly cause harm.

3. Stay in the present

There are two things you need to consider when managing your pain. The first is your perceived ability to cope with it, and the second thing is your perception of the pain's severity. If you think the pain is too great and you cannot cope, chances are your anticipation of the pain will heighten the pain itself. Stop panicking and get your mind to relax. Stay focused on each moment, because each moment will get you through the next.

These Stoic techniques help build your mental resilience as well as your endurance level. You can pair them with physical pain-relief methods like focused breathing and meditation exercises. Other things you can do to complement your efforts include journaling your pain. We know of the physical travails of Marcus Aurelius because he wrote about his experiences. This gives you a better understanding of what you are dealing with. The more understanding you have, the better equipped you are to cope with it. Medical experts also recommend maintaining a healthy lifestyle, which includes less alcohol, more exercise (which release endorphins, the body's natural painkiller), and a balanced diet.

EMOTIONAL PAIN

If you thought measuring physical pain was difficult, the complicated nature of emotional pain will leave you very confused. Saying that we are all genetically wired in different ways is stating an obvious fact, but this plays into how we handle our emotions, as well. We react to emotional traumas differently, and sometimes, our reactions to these traumas can limit our ability to function as a human being. I have had days when getting out of bed seems to be the most tasking thing I can handle. People suffering from depression may reach a point in their emotional pain when living no longer seems like a viable option. People whose emotional pain was triggered by a physical trauma describe themselves as being stuck in the place of their trauma. For them, life seems to have stopped from the very day they experienced that traumatic event. They feel frozen in time, burdened by the pain and trapped in their nightmare. This is the extent of the damage that can be caused by emotional pain.

It is very possible to experience excruciating emotional pain with no physical evidence. You can mask your pain with a smile, and that is what makes it more dangerous than physical pain. On the flip side, there are emotional pains that can manifest physically. I have heard of medical cases where the patient's emotional distress presented as a heart attack. The doctors were able to address the emergency and patch the patient up, but there are no pills or surgeries that can help you deal with the pain that is inside your head. However, if we adopt the Stoic principle that urges us to change our perspective, we can see this as a huge advantage. For starters, the absence of pills to help you get rid of your pain means that you can step into that void and be your own pill.

Being in a state of emotional pain means you are no longer in harmony with your true nature, and we know how important it is in Stoicism to maintain that balance. The obvious solution would be to restore that balance and get you back in tune with nature. Kick start the process by doing the following:

1. Accept the reality of your experience

I am not talking about amor fati or loving fate here. I am referring to the fundamental Stoic principle that tells us our experiences are neither good nor bad. Rather, they fall into the category of one of those indifferent things that are not regarded as a vice or a virtue. It is a neutral external factor that can only harm you if you let it. Yes, what happened to you is tragic and painful, and you would love for that fact to be recognized, but dwelling on it only amplifies its hold over you. This is the reality you need to awaken yourself to.

2. Recognize the limits

When we think limits, our first thought is ourselves and the boundaries that we must be conscious of. But the events around us also have their limits. They can trigger distress, cause significant pain, and temporarily create a disruption in your life—but that is as far as they can go. However tragic it was, it cannot truly harm you. Ultimately, you have the power to shut it down.

3. Take Plato's view as your stand

I love William Blake's poem, *to see a world*. When I think of Plato's view, the first verse of this poem is what comes to mind.

"To see a world in a grain of sand
And a heaven in a wildflower
Hold infinity in the palm of your hand
And eternity in an hour"

Don't narrow down your entire life's journey to this single painful moment. You have an amazing life ahead of you, and it only takes a shift in focus from the present pain to the powerful possibilities that life has to offer for you to acknowledge this. Life can take you through several twists and turns, but there is no single moment that defines you. You are the one who defines the moment.

Chapter Twenty-one
Stoicism in Growing Emotional Intelligence

"He suffers more than necessary, who suffers before it is necessary."
Seneca

If there is anything that Stoicism does, it is that it gives you a stronger sense of self. You gain a better understanding of your strengths and your weaknesses, and understand why you act the way you do. Certain traits and behavioral patterns that you exhibit will begin to make more sense as you explore this journey into yourself. More than that, you also enjoy the benefits of this process, which includes heightened confidence. A better understanding of self also goes a long way in helping you improve on the relationships in your life. However, I feel that one of the most important benefits of consistent practice of Stoicism is the insight it gives you into the feelings of others.

As the world transitioned from small, local communities to a giant global village, I think we lost touch with each other. We have become so engrossed in ourselves and in our lives that we could literally be surrounded by hundreds of people and still feel as though we live on an island that is on a planet on the dark side of the universe. Family events that are supposed to be about connecting turn into a silent communion, where the ritual involves peering into our phone screens for long hours at a time. Even intimate dinners are not spared this treatment. We no longer talk to each other, we simply talk at each other. And it is much easier to reach the person next door to you via their social media handle than by calling out their name.

When it comes to conflict resolution, our emotional intelligence is so poor that it affects our ability to see any side of the story beyond our own. Even the dissemination of information has followed the same suit. There was a time when the integrity of the journalist or writer mattered more than the stories they were telling. Before any story was published, it had to be vetted and thoroughly investigated. The truth is what was shared in the media. These days, people are more interested in making money off their stories. Sensational stories have been known to draw attention, and when you are able to draw attention, you draw the money. Therefore, priority is being given to vapid stories propped by sensational headlines, done without proper verification or investigation. And we can't place all the blame on the media—we are just as quick to share those stories with the people in our networks. And sometimes, these stories we share are so salacious and damaging for the people involved in them, but we don't give it a second thought before we spread the word.

To become emotionally intelligent, we need to apply every single Stoic principle you have learned. For starters, stop acting without thinking your actions through. When you take the time to consider every angle of the situation, your views, their views, as well as the truth, should be addressed objectively. Apply the concept of premeditation of evil to others, as well. Think of how your actions could negatively affect them. Is it worth it? Take this approach to life. Another Stoic principle that could help improve your emotional IQ would the reframing of perspectives and emotions. I cannot emphasize enough how much this has helped me in my relationships, especially in heated moments when I feel exasperated by their actions.

Our relationships with people are most vulnerable when we feel slighted or hurt. And this can happen more often than we anticipate, because another marker of the times we live in is that we have become sensitive to things that do not really matter—and, at the same time, desensitized to the things that should be important to us. We find ourselves arguing about things that have no real bearing on ourselves and walking on eggshells when it comes to topics that could shape our lives. Reframing your emotions gives you a new perspective and can make you more tolerant. Being tolerant of other people's views, behaviors, and beliefs comes from a place of emotional enlightenment.

Emotional intelligence is also reflected in how far you can push people. In our work relationships, one of the biggest issues we have—especially as leaders—is the inability to accurately assess the potentials of your colleagues. We either underutilize or over-utilize their skills. The concept of boundaries and limits is foreign to us, so we end up with employees and colleagues who are frustrated. Applying the principle of understanding limits, you are able to identify the pressure buttons of the people in your workplace, and with that information, you better understand their limits and are able to delegate tasks that motivate them enough to want to keep at it, but are still tough enough to keep them on their toes. In situations where you are unable to please people no matter what you do, using the love of fate, you can embrace the animosity in the environment and empower yourself to excel. Again, with the right perception, those challenges can be sharpened into the very tools that will bring about your advancement.

You should keep in mind that having emotional intelligence does not necessarily mean people are going to automatically like you. The objective is not to become the most liked person in the room—it is to ensure you are able to have uncomplicated and untangled relationships that are, at the very least, founded on truth and mutual respect. It is a point where the value you ascribe to people is not based on their net worth or their status in society. The same respect you accord the CEO of the company is the same respect you accord the janitor. In other words, you are not superficial in your dealings with people.

On a final note, when you use Stoicism to grow your emotional intelligence, you are able to enjoy the benefits of having people in your life without depending on them as the source of your happiness. This is a mistake we make a lot. We buy into the Hollywood notion that we need someone to complete us, and every potential relationship sets out with the goal of filling up the missing holes in our lives. The truth is, you cannot outsource your happiness. Enjoy your relationships without putting the pressure of fulfilling your happiness on them.

Chapter Twenty-two
Stoic Exercises and Practices to Get You Started

"Until we have begun to go without them, we fail to realize how unnecessary many things are.

We've been using them not because we needed them

but because we had them."

Lucius Annaeus Seneca

Most Stoic exercises, in practice, require meditation. You are to meditate on the ideas and philosophies of Stoicism so as to absorb them into your system and make them a part of you. If you have not inculcated the habit of meditation, this is something that you need to get into today. Meditation only requires your time, a quiet space, and a journal. It also requires consistency in your daily mediations. Now that we have set the tone for a Stoic lifestyle and given you an in-depth look at how Stoic principles can impact your daily living, here are a few final pointers to get you started. These are simple exercises that are more suited to a beginner, or someone seeking to reconnect with their Stoic roots. To grow and attain further enlightenment, I urge you to expand on this list. If you have been able to successfully keep at this list for at least six months, I urge you to read more books on the subjects. Books that offer excerpts or teachings based on the writings of Stoic greats like Marcus Aurelius are an excellent place to start.

For setting goals:

1. Take a pen and a notebook and write out your vision. It could be a vision for your family, your career, or even your home renovation. Don't try to raise any mental barriers, don't look at anything you feel might impede your success. Imagine that you are on a race track, with no competition on either side of you. It is just you, the empty track, and your destination. Fill those pages with your visions of the future, with no holds barred.

2. After clearly writing out your vision, use a separate sheet to write out the things that could potentially stand as obstacles—things that would either slow down your progress or threaten your vision entirely. Don't feel threatened by these obstacles. They are basically there to help you see where you should expend your energies and resources.

3. Chart the best route to achieve your goals, factoring in the obstacles you have foreseen. Ask yourself what you must do to reach your destination. If your goal is career advancement, what are the relationships you must build at work to help with that? What new skill set do you think would be relevant for the position you are aspiring for?

For growing your self-esteem:

1. Define what self-esteem means for you at this point. Would that be a more fit and healthier version of you? Or would you like to be more fashionable? Perhaps you want to be more assertive in your dealings with people. Whatever it is, write it down in clear words. If you are not sure how to begin, start your sentence with "Confidence for me means...." Complete it with exactly what you want. Try to write five or six sentences that center around what you want.

2. Objectively assess what you want and evaluate what is attainable and what isn't. Ask yourself what factors are within your control and what factors are not. Perhaps your goal is to have the body of a famous superstar. Look at your body and ask yourself if it is really achievable. If not,

opt to be healthier, instead—perhaps your goal could include losing a specific amount of weight.

3. Before you create an action plan that will lead you to your goals, start a love relationship with yourself. Write out the qualities you love about yourself, as well as qualities other people have appreciated in you. No matter how small or insignificant you think that quality is, write it out and start falling in love with yourself. Look at how well your body, your character, and your personality has served you and the other people in your life. Embrace that—and only when you are comfortable with that should you advance to creating a plan to become the most confident version of yourself.

For becoming more generous or giving [philanthropy]:

1. Start this process by meditating on your perception of other people. In order to become more deliberate with the distribution of your wealth—be it time, money, or knowledge—you have to first start thinking of people as an extension of yourself. As long as people remain strangers to you, you will be unable to care

enough to genuinely become concerned about their well-being.

2. Look at the tethers that bind you to your possessions. We are typically unable to give because we have formed unhealthy attachments to the things we own. Remind yourself that nothing is forever. You may never fit into that shirt you are holding onto, so why not give it to someone who can benefit from it right now? Also, apply some meditation of evil in this process. If you were to suddenly lose everything, how well would that serve you or the people around you? This helps you detach yourself from the things you own. Enjoy the benefits they bring you, but don't attach any value to them.

3. Gift someone without prompting. If, at first, the process feels weird, you can start by giving those closest to you a gift. It could be a quick phone call that just focuses on their well-being, where you listen and offer the support they need. Find out how they are doing, what is going on in their lives. Spend a few hours with your grandparents. Do the odd chore around the house, or just sit down and chat. Volunteer at your local soup kitchen. It may feel a bit strange, initially, but keep at it on a monthly or weekly basis. Saying hello to a random stranger and

paying them a compliment are also daily or weekly tasks you could assign yourself.

Chapter Twenty-three
Taking Ownership of Your Life

"Most powerful is he who has himself in his own power."

Seneca

If you have spent your life blaming the rest of the world for any perceived injustice, you might never be able to make any real progress. Yes, what has happened to you may have been cruel and unfair, but the power that the person or persons in question had over you ended the day or the period in which they inflicted that hurt or trauma. The moment you stepped outside of that, the power reverted back to you. And, right now, I am not referring to the general talk about the negative energy that surrounds one's inability to forgive, although that does have its own type of emotional poison. I am talking about subjecting yourself subconsciously to hurt over and over again. Except this time around, you are holding in your own hands the weapon that is inflicting the pain.

Throughout this book, the underlying message has been that the ultimate power to transform our lives and to live the life we desire is in us. And all you have to do is reach out and take that power. Of course, to do it the Stoic way, your first hurdle would have to be overhauling the years of thinking patterns and behaviors that you have learned throughout your lifetime. This process is not easy, but it is not complicated, either. In a few paragraphs, I am going to go over certain thinking pillars that you will need to break down so these new principles you are trying to imbibe can inform the decisions that you make. This is not a complete list, but it covers the basics. As you evolve, you will make new discoveries. Include those discoveries in your own list.

1. You are responsible.

When we hear a phrase like that, we think in terms of obligations and duties. We think of specific tasks that fall within the purview of what we feel is our "job description." In this new life, being responsible goes beyond your daily chores or the duties assigned to you in your role as a wife, husband, parent, friend, or employee. It means you are the main agent for everything that happens in your life. This is huge, especially if you have always believed that everything that has happened to you up until now is the work of divine power. But here is the truth: That divine power still exists and, in the grand scheme of things, there are events that have been designed just for you. However, you are the one who defines those experiences. So, if you want to explore your full potential, you need to accept that you are the one responsible for the choices, actions, and experiences in your life.

2. You should expect the terrible stuff to happen to you.

Put this way, it does sound like a horrible thing to say, but these are some of the things you are going to have to psychologically prepare yourself for. When you face the future, don't just look for the white fluffy clouds, the pot of gold at the end of the rainbow, and the unicorn. There will be dragons and darkness and things we would rather were not there, but denying their existence will not make them cease to exist. Instead, see these things as necessary tools to fast-track your process to living the good life. Your power lies in your ability to use both the good and the bad stuff to your advantage.

3. Your idea of what is good and what is bad is skewered.

There are true virtues, as you have learned, and there are also vices. But what is classified as good or bad are actually known as either preferred indifferent or disliked indifferent. That awesome job you love so much is a preferred indifferent, and losing that job would be defined as disliked indifferent. That job has benefits that, to an extent, help you maintain your dignity as it pays your bills, keeps you fed, and clothed. So you would rather have a job than not. However, it does not affect your virtue because if you were to lose it tomorrow, you could still find happiness. In other words, a lot of the things you have held close to your heart as the things that defined your life and well-being are actually just positive contributors. They are placeholders for the real thing, until you are able to get to that place where you understand the true value of your own thoughts. Your power or sense of self-worth is not in the things you desire.

4. Your experience is essentially what you permit.

This goes along the same line as you being responsible, but I had to create a separate section for this because many of us have been through experiences that our peers cannot even begin to imagine. And often, we feel these experiences justify the pain we live with daily. We make mistakes that come with grievous consequences, and we cannot get past the pain we have caused others. So, we feel that by punishing ourselves, we can in some way atone for them. These are lies that we tell ourselves to help us feel better about what has happened, but the feeling is temporary, and we continue this cycle of self-hurt. The things that people have done to you have no power over you. Just like the mistakes that you have made have no power over you. This is a concept that you will struggle with, especially if you the voices around you have been echoing your thoughts. Embrace fate, and everything that has happened, and you embrace your potential to be more.

I can write 50 books on the Stoic principles, and Seneca himself can rise up from his grave to mentor you on this very subject, but if you are unable to admit these basic truths and accept the powers that come with them, there is a distinct possibility that you will not be able to live out your full potential, much less reach the goals of being more confident, living more consciously, and enjoying the good life. There are no walls, no barriers or persons that can stop you from living your best life. As they say, the only person capable of standing in the way of your success is you. And that is because you hold the ultimate power.

James W. Williams

Closing

I would like to leave you with these wise words from one of Stoicism's greatest masters, Seneca:

"Let us prepare our minds as if we'd come to the very end of life. Let us postpone nothing. Let us balance life's books each day... the one who puts the finishing touches on their life each day is never short of time."

We typically live our lives trying valiantly to postpone our meeting with death. We want to live forever—a noble concept, but leaves us with the fear of tomorrow. Among a group of friends, the subject of mortality came up. I found out that a lot of us are more enthusiastic about the afterlife. We hold onto the prospect of going to heaven and, obviously, nobody wants to make their bed in hell. We talked about living a life on earth that makes us worthy of heaven. One of our more mischievous companions asked the question: if the proverbial trumpets rang out today and the call to all saints to go to heaven was made, would you willing leave everything behind and answer that call?

Stoicism

A deadly hush fell upon the table. This was followed by a loud clearing of throats and uncomfortable laughs. Not one person was ready to face death, even after they had just portrayed heaven as this wonderful place. You see, there was no questioning the existence of heaven or hell—that was not the real issue. The issue was that many of us are tethered to earth, despite our pious affiliation and devotion to heaven. There is nothing wrong with that, either. Only that, for a group of people who are clueless as to when death will inevitably come, we sure take living for granted.

The Stoic way of living prepares you for the inevitability of death while ensuring you live your life to the fullest. The uncertainty of tomorrow should not stop you from living now, and just because you are living now doesn't mean you should not pay any attention to tomorrow. Live right, with the people you surround yourself with. Do things that give you a sense of purpose, in that you are playing your part in the universal scheme of things. Take everything life arms you with and turn it into a bestseller that will be your life. That is what this book is all about.

Epictetus described life as "hard, brutal, punishing, narrow and confining, a deadly business." Stoicism is meant to help you make sense of your journey. With it, you'll find strength in the face of adversity, discover the opportunities in your obstacles, and attain a perspective that sees you rising above your pain.

Thank you

Before you go, I just wanted to say thank you for purchasing my book.

You could have picked from dozens of other books on the same topic, but you chose this one.

So, a HUGE thanks to you for getting this book and for reading all the way to the end.

Now, I wanted to ask you for a small favor. **Could you please consider posting a review on the platform? Reviews are one of the easiest ways to support the work of authors.**

This feedback will help me continue to write the type of books that will help you get the results you want. So, if you enjoyed it, please let me know.

Lastly, don't forget to grab a copy of your Free Bonus book *"Bulletproof Confidence Checklist."* If you want to learn how to overcome shyness and social anxiety and become more confident, then this book is for you.
Just go to:
https://theartofmastery.com/confidence/

www.ingramcontent.com/pod-product-compliance
Lightning Source LLC
Chambersburg PA
CBHW071714020426
42333CB00017B/2270